GOOD
PEOPLE

GOOD PEOPLE

Stories From the
Best of Humanity

GABRIEL REILICH & LUCIA KNELL

Illustrations by Libby VanderPloeg

WASHINGTON, D.C.

Published by National Geographic Partners, LLC
1145 17th Street NW Washington, DC 20036

Library of Congress Cataloging-in-Publication Data
Names: Knell, Lucia, editor. | Reilich, Gabriel, editor. | VanderPloeg, Libby, illustrator.
Title: Upworthy good people : stories from the best of humanity / [edited by] Lucia Knell &
    Gabriel Reilich ; illustrations by Libby VanderPloeg.
Description: Washington, D.C. : National Geographic Partners, [2024] | Summary: "This
    heartwarming collection of first-person tales from Upworthy will provide comfort and
    inspiration to anyone who could use a dose of joy"-- Provided by publisher.
Identifiers: LCCN 2023033909 (print) | LCCN 2023033910 (ebook) |
    ISBN 9781426223464 (hardcover) | ISBN 9781426224263 (ebook)
Subjects: LCSH: Joy. | Kindness. | Compassion.
Classification: LCC BF575.H27 U69 2024 (print) | LCC BF575.H27 (ebook) | DDC
    158--dc23/eng/20230830
LC record available at https://lccn.loc.gov/2023033909
LC ebook record available at https://lccn.loc.gov/2023033910

Since 1888, the National Geographic Society has funded more than 14,000 research, conservation, education, and storytelling projects around the world. National Geographic Partners
distributes a portion of the funds it receives from your purchase to National Geographic
Society to support programs including the conservation of animals and their habitats.

Get closer to National Geographic Explorers and photographers, and connect with our
global community. Join us today at nationalgeographic.org/joinus

For rights or permissions inquiries, please contact National Geographic Books Subsidiary
Rights: bookrights@natgeo.com

Interior design: Elisa Gibson

ISBN: 978-1-4262-2346-4

Printed in Malaysia

24/IVM/1

To humanity—big fans

CONTENTS

Introduction

Every day on Upworthy, we work to shine a light on the best of humanity. Over the years we've grown an online community of millions—of all ages, from all corners of the world—who share in our core belief that people are fundamentally good. Our posts inspire an outpouring of comments from our readers, each with their own heartfelt narrative. Reading through them is the best part of our jobs, because so many prove our mission. But the nature of social media can make it hard to find them again. They get lost, buried under an avalanche of content. That didn't sit right with us. These comments—each the seed of a beautiful story—deserved more.

So, we began to pose questions to our community with a greater sense of curiosity and intention. Questions like "What's the kindest thing a stranger has ever done for you?" We were met with thousands of replies—stories, wisdom, truths, and triumphs—each a privileged glimpse into people's minds, hearts, and lives.

Energized and inspired, we asked a select number of followers to participate in a new project, an experiment of sorts—one that would grow the seeds of their stories, their comments, into something more permanent. A book. We set out to create a counterbalance to the darker forces and algorithms fighting for our attention. Something to provide readers with space for the quiet, contemplative, and restorative calm we all need.

We pored over these stories dozens of times. Themes began to reveal themselves, which then became the six chapters of this book. And every time we read them—every single time—we were moved. Maybe that's just how goodness works. Its power doesn't diminish with contact. Instead, it grows and grows.

Our hope is that this book will serve as a resource for comfort: 101 stories you can turn to again and again, each page a reassurance that people, more often than not, are good at heart. They are funny, moving, surprising, heartbreaking, inspiring, and, most of all, real. We are forever grateful to all who opened up and contributed these meaningful pieces of their lives, large and small.

The truth is, the book of human decency continues to be written every day. Let's all keep adding stories to it together.

—Gabriel Reilich and Lucia Knell

GOOD
PEOPLE

CHAPTER ONE

The Kindest of Strangers

There are a lot of good people out there

Safe Travels

AMY B.

I t's sort of an East Coast thing—a rite of passage—moving to
New York. I grew up in a suburb outside D.C. Relative to New
York, D.C. is amateur hour. So, when I got into Cardozo—a
young, progressive law school in New York—I didn't hesitate.
Goodbye, small potatoes. Hello, Big Apple.

In the grand tradition of moving to New York, I was just 22—
naive enough not to think of myself as naive—and wholly unwor-
ried about dangers that may lay in store. You know, the kind people
warn you about—pickpockets, subway creeps, lurkers in the park.

In fact, my instincts were correct. In 2010, New York bore little
resemblance to the gritty cesspool represented in *Taxi Driver* and
The Panic in Needle Park; that brand of trepidation belonged to
people who'd never actually lived here. The danger ahead was of an
entirely different variety. The kind that visits you no matter where
you live. The kind that arrives politely—a phone call, a knock on
the door—and casually blows up your life.

My boyfriend—a soon-to-be relic of my past—dropped me off.
I remember it so clearly—standing there in the cold, my suitcase
at my side like a comrade, my own R2-D2. The taillights of my
boyfriend's car receded, glowed brighter, turned a corner, and disappeared. It was January 4 and 17 degrees Fahrenheit—so it's fair to
say the moment is frozen in time.

I lived in "intern housing" for five months—the average amount
of time required to secure an apartment that is both affordable and
doesn't resemble a Soviet-era interrogation room. Intern housing
turned out to be the New Yorker Hotel, which was terribly cool to
me at the time. Cardozo had reserved an entire floor for students
and interns from all over the world. Before long, I was doing things
like walking briskly to the subway, Greek coffee cup in hand, giving

tourists directions and skirting dead rats with aplomb. I was, at last, a bona fide New Yorker (or at least someone who could be mistaken for one).

Of course, I still called my parents. A lot. I even listened to bedtime stories. Technically.

My dad and I both loved reading. He was always giving me books, talking to me about books—and now, reading aloud lengthy paragraphs from books over the phone. He always wanted to talk about it—the story and the writing and the symbolism—and how it made him think and feel. I loved it. I'll never forget the pride I felt the first time I recommended a book my dad enjoyed in the same way I enjoyed books he recommended to me. Perhaps—even more so than moving to New York, going to law school, and keeping a houseplant alive—successfully recommending a book to my dad made me realize I'd made it. At long last, I was an adult.

> When I turned my phone on again, the screen lit up with a dozen missed calls—all from my mom.

I woke up that morning racked with nerves. It was the first day of my clinical internship— January 27, 2012—my final semester of law school. I chose my outfit carefully—black pantsuit, pale blue buttondown, sensible heels—then showed up to discover it was a casual office, everyone in jeans and T-shirts. The rest of the day was dull, boredom breaking only once, in the middle of orientation, when my phone went off like a nuclear meltdown alarm. Embarrassed for the second time that day, I turned it off and apologized. When I turned it on again, at 5 p.m., the screen lit up with a dozen missed calls—all from my mom. I knew something was wrong. She picked up on the first ring.

"Just so you know," I said. "I'm in an elevator with someone else."

I'll put it this way: When I entered the elevator, I was one person; when I exited, I was someone else. Sometimes I look back and imagine the "someone else" in that elevator was me—the version of me that would never receive this call, the version that emerged from the elevator's sliding doors to walk through the lobby, hail a cab, and meet friends for drinks. Maybe she's out there somewhere, living my parallel life—the one in which my dad didn't die suddenly of a heart attack.

My friend Jess was already waiting outside the building. The second I saw her, I collapsed. Poor Jess—she's really tiny—and yet, somehow, she managed to practically carry me the three blocks to my apartment. My childhood best friend met us there. She and Jess packed my suitcase. I was so out of it, I couldn't even recall where my clothes were. As though clothes belonged to some other realm in which people had bodies to clothe. I had no body. I was a vapor, the puff of smoke after the rabbit disappears.

My dad was an artist. The house always smelled like paint, or sounded like whatever tools he was using. A hammer could actually be soothing, so strongly did I associate it with him. He was always listening to music. He had a motorcycle that shook the whole house when he started it up in the garage. When my friends put me in that cab to LaGuardia, I was sobbing so hard I couldn't hear. And I'd discover a short while later that people don't die all at once. It's more like an earthquake, with endless rolling aftershocks; even years later, when the aftershocks mostly subside, you'll find it difficult to adapt, like a sailor on steady ground. My father died the first time when my mother told me so over the phone. He'd die again when I got home to a house bereft of certain sounds.

I got through security, somehow, and sat on the floor against a wall, my phone plugged into the outlet. I called a friend to see if he could pick me up when I arrived—my mother couldn't drive. After that, I just sat there, pitiful, crying. According to social contract, no one noticed—or rather, everyone pretended not to notice.

And yet, someone did stop. He might as well have been the Man in the Gray Flannel Suit, he was so nondescript—a 40-something commuter of average height, dressed in a button-down tucked into work slacks, holding a briefcase. "Are you OK?" he asked. "Do you need anything? Are you by yourself?"

It's funny in retrospect, because my dad would have been super mad knowing I told this strange man in the airport—"Yes! I am all by myself." But I took it one step further and told him my whole sad situation—I was flying home, my dad had just died, I'd bought the earliest flight I could, but it wasn't leaving for hours and I got to the airport super early.

The man took all this in with a look of concern—sincere, authoritative concern, like President Obama in the Situation Room.

He told me to wait where I was: Not a problem, because I was as attached to that wall as my phone charger. When he returned—it could have been five minutes, or 50—he told me he got me on an earlier flight. It wasn't a lot earlier, but the smallest amount of time mattered so much to me. I was taken aback by this unexpected

act of generosity, even in my current state. I don't remember his name—I'm not sure he even told me his name. I didn't know what he did for a living. And yet, he carried my bag to the gate, sat across the aisle from me, and held my hand. He asked me questions. He asked about my dad. He talked to me that entire flight, and when we landed, he walked me all the way to the door to where my best friend from high school picked me up. I think he waved goodbye. I'm not sure I thanked him—I hope so.

Like my father's death, this anonymous act of compassion changed me forever. I'm less afraid to approach the crying girl on the street to ask, "Are you OK?" I haven't saved any lives, or counseled anyone through grief. But I have made friends for the night. I don't walk by, pretending not to see.

If I were to cross paths with that man today, I wonder would I recognize him? When I think of his face, it's a total blank. It was his kindness that left the indelible impression.

I was so young—24—when I lost my dad. None of my friends could relate. For years I felt really alone—stranded on my planet for one. I still feel that way sometimes. But I think about the man who helped me that day—every time I'm at a gate, every time a plane takes off, every time I'm looking for my ride. I don't feel alone when I fly. His kindness keeps me company. ∎

SPOTLIGHT

My sister and I were visiting Chicago and trying to get our crappy, out-dated luggage up some steps. Some random guy came over, grabbed them, and pulled them up the rest of the way. I'll never forget his reply when we said thank you: "Live to give." That's been my mantra ever since.
—*Sarah Beth R. T.*

The Art of Parenting

ERICA T.

One thing about motherhood people don't talk about enough is the way we have to Pretend That Everything Is Fine, No Matter What. It's a survival skill that begins the minute a tiny stranger is placed in your arms and you realize:

1. No one taught you how to be a mom.
2. You and your baby may be totally screwed.
3. It's too late to cram him back in there.

So, you pretend! Everything's fine and totally under control, guys! *I got this.* You smile even when you're scared shitless, and, eventually, your baby starts smiling back. That's motherhood.

When Kieran was two years old, he was a blond-haired, blue-eyed bundle of energy—still babyish with chubby arms and legs but running around like a big kid. My divorce was almost final, thank goodness, but it was messy and awful, and I was exhausted. I had sole custody, which I wanted. But being a single parent is a lot.

We went to the Phoenix Art Museum one morning, just to get out of the house. I love art—I'm an artist, after all—and walking through the exhibits, especially in the morning right after they open, soothes me. Kieran was happily exploring the area between the walls and the wide wooden handrails, running his hands through the empty spaces, when suddenly his arm got stuck.

Now, I don't know how long we stood there while I pretended not to freak out. His arm was wedged so tightly that no amount of maneuvering was working, and I definitely didn't want him to realize he was stuck. I couldn't leave to get help, and because we were there so early in the day, no one else was around to assist.

In that moment I realized how very alone we were in the

world, both literally and figuratively. Everything was falling apart. I couldn't support us. I couldn't handle any of this. He would be trapped there forever. Maybe we could just live here in the museum. Maybe we could become an exhibit.

As I silently panicked, my mom-face defaulted into a happy, brave, *everything is fine* smile. Kieran wiggled a bit, but remained calmly curious about his predicament. I noticed his eyes dart to something behind me—I turned around. There was the most beautiful man I've ever seen: ethereal and otherworldly, calm and collected.

He was wearing a solid white dashiki that made him glow, and he spoke with a heavy accent. A group of equally beautiful, similarly dressed people walked with him, and collectively they had this cool, chilled-out vibe that seemed to fill the air. In my mind I was thinking crazy thoughts like, *This is an angel but angels aren't real, so what the hell is happening?!* But on the outside, I just stood there, gaping. The man leaned over, whispered something into my son's ear, and popped his arm out like magic. And then it was over. A stranger had transformed us from museum captives to regular attendees in a matter of seconds. We were free.

> So, you pretend! Everything's fine and totally under control, guys! *I got this.*

I'm not a hugger, especially with strangers, but I asked the man who helped Kieran if I could hug him because I was so thankful for his help, and he, in his infinite kindness, obliged. That serene intervention was exactly what I needed at exactly the right time, and it drove home the following realizations:

1. Even when it feels like I'm completely alone, I'm not.
2. Just because I can't see a way out doesn't mean there isn't one.
3. Art museums have to make *everything* artsy, even their damn handrails. ∎

Do It for Peggy

MIKE A.

P eggy was a train attendant, but I like to refer to her as St. Peggy, patron saint of smiles. I met her while visiting Toronto with my boyfriend. We took the train into the city, and Peggy was the attendant checking our tickets. After she clipped them, she stood and talked with us for a while. Every few sentences, she would smile or laugh, and immediately, we would smile and laugh, too. I'm telling you, it was weirdly contagious.

We talked to her for less than 10 minutes, but I swear, she changed my life. I've never met someone whose presence struck me so strongly. She was joy personified. When the train reached our stop and we walked down the platform, we both glanced back. There she was, waving at us from the window, wishing us safe travels.

Since that day, my boyfriend and I have coined the phrase "Do it for Peggy," which we exclaim when we need to do something challenging.

Moving a mattress down the hallway? Do it for Peggy! Have to get a root canal? Do it for Peggy!

Headed to a family reunion, a funeral, or the Department of Motor Vehicles? You know what to do. Do it for Peggy. See? You can't help but smile. ∎

All the Good in the World

KAREN B.

There's a motto often repeated inside the rooms of Alcoholics Anonymous: We suffer to get well. It means, of course, that pain drives us to the point of being desperate enough to change. To do the scary thing. To stop drinking. To ask for help.

Alcoholics don't like pain, and we sure as hell don't like to suffer. That's how I ended up drinking in the first place.

I grew up in Seattle, where my best friend and I used to walk around our neighborhood smoking cigarettes and trying to look cool. At age 12, we caught the eye of a creep, who regularly offered us cups of peach schnapps in exchange for letting him smack us on the ass. At the time, this seemed like a fair trade.

Alcohol provided an escape I desperately craved after an unsettled and challenging childhood. From then on, I didn't do anything sober if I could help it, and it stayed that way for more than two decades.

I was working as a limo driver the night my life took an abrupt turn. My assignment was simple: Pick up a bride and groom at the church where their wedding took place and drive them a short distance to their hotel. Easy enough, right?

My drinking was way out of hand by that point. By the time I showed up to work, I'd already begun to black out, so I don't remember any of this, but, before I went to the church, I sideswiped a gas pump after filling up the limo's tank, causing a bunch of property damage and catching a hit-and-run charge.

I arrived at the church with scratches all down the side of my limousine, loaded up the happy couple, and … refused to take them to their hotel. We went on a joyride instead! I thought it would be fun, but apparently they did not see it that way and I was charged with kidnapping and driving under the influence. The company I worked for offered to drop the charges if I went to rehab, and I agreed to go without hesitation. That option certainly sounded more appealing than serving jail time.

Rehab is where I found the love of my life.

Pat had the brightest blue eyes I'd ever seen, the color of the Caribbean Sea. Just looking at him felt like a three-week vacation. I remember sitting in an AA meeting, holding my shiny coin representing 30 days of continuous sobriety, and wondering, Who is that good-looking man? Was he really that happy? How anyone could find happiness without alcohol, I had no idea. I, for one, was miserable. But when Pat smiled, his whole face lit up and those blue eyes beamed even brighter. I needed to get to know him, which meant both of us would need to stay sober.

I kept showing up, day after day, and so did he.

The people in recovery who watched our relationship bloom said we didn't have a chance in hell to stay sober if we got together; we were both severe alcoholics who could barely take care of ourselves, let alone another person. But we did. We hung on for dear life, to our sobriety and to each other. Nine months later, I left rehab, moved into a small house, and started building a real life. Pat moved in, too, and he never left.

For 25 sober years, Pat and I were married, living a free-spirited, nomadic lifestyle. Both of us were loners, happy to depend on each other for support and companionship, content to hang out at home and dedicate our time to our work and each other. When one of us felt like we wanted a drink, the other one was there to say, "That's a terrible idea." We never wavered. He was my best friend, and those bright blue eyes continued to slay me. I never got tired of looking at them.

When Pat died suddenly of an aortic aneurysm at the age of 63,

I found myself completely and totally alone—in a very rural area, surrounded by cow pastures and farms. Overnight, I didn't have anyone. The grief was unspeakable.

Of the many hurdles I've had to overcome since becoming a widow, the hardest arrived upon realizing I had no one to drive me to the hospital for a medical procedure. The doctor required me to be accompanied by someone. But who? I weighed my options for days, trying to figure out how to make it work.

I was chatting with another woman online who lived in Sweden. She asked if I'd considered posting about my predicament in the local Neighbors Helping Neighbors Facebook group.

"Really? Ask a total stranger?" I asked, appalled at the idea.

Three days before my appointment, however, the pressure was on. I mustered up all my courage and posted a call for help. I've never felt more vulnerable in my entire life. Not only was my appointment in Kansas City, more than an hour away, but I needed someone to drive me there, stay with me, and drive me home. I was asking for someone to give up an entire day. For me! And I'm a small-boned, 61-year-old widow with chronic pain. What if someone tried to take advantage of me?

> Pat had the brightest blue eyes I'd ever seen, the color of the Caribbean Sea. Just looking at him felt like a three-week vacation.

I walked away from my computer feeling physically sick over the whole situation. I missed Pat.

Hours later, I returned to my computer to discover so many people offering to help that tears started streaming down my face. The outpouring of kindness was just unbelievable; it felt like a warm blanket. One woman in particular took the time to send a private message explaining who she was and how she had the day off and would be happy to contribute. She seemed trustworthy and reliable, so I agreed to let her take me.

During the ride, I found out she lived with three developmentally challenged adults and worked as their caretaker. This was her only, much needed day off, and she chose to use it to help me.

I choked back tears as we chatted like old friends; she was so kind and sweet, and my heart was so broken over losing Pat. I'd been alone for so many months—just being around another human demonstrating such empathy did more for me than any pain medicine ever could. After she brought me home, she continued to check in and reminded me that she was around if I ever needed her.

The experience reminded me that there are still good people in the world if you're willing to open yourself up to them. And, maybe, in the midst of all my suffering, I'm also starting to heal. ∎

SPOTLIGHT

Years ago, I overpurchased; my car wasn't big enough to hold a dining table and four chairs. A nice woman with a small child saw me struggling. She offered to put the items in her van and had her child ride with me. We got to my new apartment, and she helped carry everything up two flights! I have never forgotten her kindness. —*Lisa S.*

Sky's the Limit

BRITTNEY F.

I graduated from the University of Texas at Austin with a bachelor's in government, so as you can imagine, I had been rigorously prepared for my first job out of college—waiting tables at the Cheesecake Factory.

I'm the oldest of four girls and spent the greater part of my life raising little sisters. When I was 14, my father was sentenced to a 99-year prison sentence; less than a year later, my mother, who struggled with substance abuse, left. Rather than let their failures deter me, I worked even harder, finishing high school and college. I wanted to show my sisters I could do it, so they would be inspired to do the same.

Unfortunately, I graduated college in December 2008—right smack in the middle of the Great Recession—so jobs were pretty tough to come by. I was lucky to have any job; I knew that. Still, I wanted a bigger slice of that proverbial pie—just not a literal cheesecake.

Desperate for advice, I visited an old UT professor and pled my case. He told me to go to law school. "People in my family aren't lawyers—they need lawyers," I retorted. "Brittney," he replied, "you don't even need to practice law with that degree. Just having it already opens up so many doors." I thought of my sisters. We needed open doors.

When I got home, I booked an LSAT test. I studied hard on my own, and when I sat for the test, scored 158 out of 180. It was an "OK" score, but I needed a great one to get into a competitive school. I looked into test prep courses—I knew they gave people an edge—but that came at a price: $1,200, to be exact. I'd need to clock in 165 hours to cover the cost—and that's not factoring in living expenses. No way could I afford that.

I went to bed feeling like I'd been stabbed in the heart. It wasn't fair. I wanted to go to school again.

On one particularly glum Sunday morning, I wove through the restaurant, pitcher in hand, summoning up every ounce of will to smile. Among the tables, I noticed Sky, one of our regulars, sitting alone in an old dress, her gray hair swept into a low bun. I filled her glass, and the smile we exchanged was genuine. It was nice, not having to make an effort. I walked back into the kitchen, leaned against the walk-in, and closed my eyes.

"Brit," a co-worker said. I opened my eyes. "Sky was just talking about law school. You wanna do that, right? You should talk to her."

It was a slow morning—none of the managers were working. I decided that would be a good idea, to have that conversation. "Sky," I said. "Can I sit with you a little while?"

"Of course, sweetie."

"I heard you know a lot about law school. I was wondering, do you know anything about applying?"

Sky told me that, some years prior, she'd opened an accounting firm with her husband. It was so successful in the last year that she'd decided to follow an enduring dream of practicing law. She signed up for an LSAT prep class, fully intending to take the exam, when, tragically, her husband died. So she decided to pursue an MBA instead—a skill more relevant to the firm. "I recommend taking a prep course, 100 percent," she said.

Her kindness put me at ease and encouraged me to open up about my childhood. "I know I can't get into the best schools with the scores I have now," I said. "But those courses are out of my league, financially speaking." Sky nodded her head as I spoke. "Everything will work out," she said. "I'm sure of it."

Recharged by her empathy, I got up and went back to work, refilling ice water and delivering Factory specials. "Here you go, sir!" I chirped, presenting an enormous order of fettuccine Alfredo. The dish clinked on the table, wide noodles sprawled across the plate like my underutilized, college-educated brain.

> Sometimes it feels like life is stacked against you: a tower of dirty dishes piled high in a restaurant sink. Other times, it feels like life's a friend you didn't know you had.

A few days later, Sky returned—another old dress, same gray bun, sitting at her habitual booth.

I greeted her with a big smile. But before I could speak, she interrupted.

"I want to give you my prep course."

My eyes widened.

"I already paid for it." She put up a hand, shooting down potential protest. "They're tellin' me it's 'not allowed' for me to transfer it over to you. But I'll figure it out."

And she did. I finished the prep course that summer and took the LSAT the following fall. My score jumped from a 158 to a 167, which put me in the top 93 percent, which in turn got me into

Boston College Law School. I graduated cum laude in 2013, moved back to Texas, and passed the bar, leaving me with only one, final hurdle: I had to choose between corporate law or public service law. I chose the latter because of Sky.

Sometimes it feels like life is stacked against you: a tower of dirty dishes piled high in a restaurant sink. Other times, it feels like life's a friend you didn't know you had—a sweet, older woman in a booth at the Cheesecake Factory who decides to help you achieve your dreams. Because of Sky, I'm no longer shackled to that restaurant, unable to move forward. Instead, I'm a lawyer—working hard for the people. As a rule, I strive to emulate Sky by listening to and supporting my clients, giving them a fighting chance in this world. ▪

SPOTLIGHT

Was on my weekly date night with my five-year-old having fun chatting and eating. When I received the bill, another table had paid it and said to tell me that I'm a really good mother. —*Daphne F.*

Raising Hell

KELLY S.

I live in Missoula, Montana, which once upon a time went by another name. Numerous battles between Indigenous tribes had littered the valley with human bones, inspiring French fur trappers to call the place La Porte de l'Enfer: the Gate of Hell.

Every time I went to work, I just thought, Yep, that sounds about right.

You see, my boss wasn't exactly the nicest guy. Which is, of course, my nice way of saying he was an asshole. Like, borderline abusive. Gaslighting, constant criticism, explosive rage, the works. The kind of personality you'd associate with a Hollywood mogul or a mob boss. Not a dentist.

Anyway, every devil needs a henchman, and that was me—his assistant. Guardian of dental instruments. Wrangler of suction tubes. I stood by him as he filled cavities and performed root canals, sniped petty comments and bellowed orders. I stood by him, but I couldn't stand him. The whine of the drill haunts me still. The countless extracted teeth made for a new valley littered with bones. I'd soak up all his anger, carry it around with me all day, go home, and cry. Every day was like this. Lather, rinse, repeat.

> Every devil needs a henchman, and that was me—his assistant. Guardian of dental instruments. Wrangler of suction tubes.

Every couple of months or so, I was treated to a break in this routine with a trip to Costco, where I would go to restock the office supplies. Towers of toilet paper, a two-month supply of bleach—my cart looked like it belonged to someone cleaning a murder scene. (Which, in a way, I was—the double homicide of my sanity and my self-esteem.) The dentist didn't set aside time for this errand—I used my lunch hour—so these trips were inevitably rushed and stressful.

That day, it was particularly bad. I pushed my rattling, overburdened cart across the parking lot, barely balancing my "Leaning Tower of TP," when I hit a speed bump and it all came crashing down.

Remember all the anger I soaked up every day? Well, it erupted, right there in the Costco parking lot. I was a veritable geyser of bile: cussing, spewing, gnashing my teeth, snatching packs of toilet paper off the ground, attempting to reconstruct a second tower with quaking hands. It kept collapsing. The only thing I was capable of building, it seemed, was rage.

Worse than the rage, though, was the shame. I didn't want to be this person. I felt so embarrassed, so exposed—a pustule of a human being, a troll banished from decent society—which was why, when a woman broke away from her cart to run toward me, rather than away, I was stunned. "Oh, honey!" she said. "Let me help."

By the time we got to my car, I could barely hold back tears. I knew if I said something, I'd lose it—a fact she clearly intuited by giving me space, but filling it, too, with compassion and understanding. When we finished loading the trunk, I managed to choke out a thank-you. She smiled, meeting my eyes, like maybe I wasn't a troll after all, but a person.

I'm happy to report I no longer work for the dentist. I quit sometime later, shortly after his office manager of 30 years left, citing "horrible work conditions."

I wonder, sometimes, if I hadn't crossed paths with that woman in the Costco parking lot—if I hadn't encountered a kindness that threw the dentist's cruelty into stark relief—if I would have stayed in that office another 30 years, too. But I didn't. And I have her to thank for that. ∎

The Unlikely Sentinel

ANNABELLA M.

I t was winter, the time of year folks burrowed into their homes and swaddled themselves in blankets while stoking the fire. That was my plan, too—as soon as I could get there. I'd have to make a 45-minute drive first.

I locked my shop door with frozen fingers and trudged uphill to my car. Damp air slapped sharply from all directions and a foreboding dark descended. I had to hurry. When I reached the top of the hill, I saw my parked car, silver against the gray sky. I walked faster now, anticipating the refuge of that driver's seat, the hot air blowing on my feet.

By now, it was entirely dark, the narrow, desolate country lanes only dimly and sporadically lit. Hail began to come down, loudly hammering the surface of the car. As I turned onto a road I'd driven a hundred times before, I noticed there were no street-lights, transforming the shrubbery on either side of the road into tall, dark walls.

All at once, the hail came down with greater force. Ice battered my car, drowning the radio, cracking the windshield. Then, in a moment that lasted a thousand moments, I lost control of my car. Gripping the wheel, I braced myself for impact, strangely attuned to minute details—for instance, two tiny blinking headlights in the distance. If they'd been just a little bit closer, I thought, our cars would have collided.

My car hit the tall, dark wall of shrubbery. The impact was forceful, but not painful—the seat belt did its job. A massive cracking noise ripped through the car. When everything became still, my hands unstuck from the wheel, shaking uncontrollably.

I dialed my husband's number, relaying the accident with barely decipherable words. He was on his way.

Placing the phone in my lap, I once again noticed the headlights—no longer tiny, blinking lights, but large and close. Then, an indicator, orange and flashing, as the car pulled closer to mine. The car door opened, illuminating a man's face—square jaw, ginger hair. He got out of his car, straightened his jacket, covered his head with his hood, and walked tentatively over the muddy, icy ground.

"Are you OK?" he asked gently through my closed window, hands thrust into his pockets. I looked up at him through the streaky window, nodded.

"Is someone coming for you?"

"Yes. My husband."

"OK, good."

He looked around, then back at me. "I'm going to sit and wait in my car over there," he said in the same reassuring voice. "Until your husband comes."

"Oh no," I said. "Thank you so much. But I can't ask you to do that. He's 45 minutes away."

> We sat there, he in his car, me in mine, lights faintly illuminating our driver's seats in the dark.

He dismissed my words gently, shaking his head, and retreated to his car—throwing a thumbs-up. I smiled, too grateful to argue. Shortly after, I realized the hail had stopped and half expected him to drive off. He didn't. We sat there, he in his car, me in mine, lights faintly illuminating our driver's seats in the dark.

I sank into my coat and listened to the radio. On the couple occasions I looked to my left, I noticed my strangely comforting companion, head tilted down, looking at his phone. From what I could tell, he didn't look at me at all—which I realized later was just one of many subtle ways he made me feel so safe. When my husband finally arrived, after first checking to see I was OK, he lifted his chin to both greet and thank the young man in the car—who'd already turned on his engine to leave. He acknowledged our gratitude with a soft smile and a raised palm. And then he drove away.

The young man must have introduced himself, but I don't remember his name. But I'll never forget him—my unlikely sentinel. My light in the dark. Memories of his kindness warm me still. ∎

SPOTLIGHT

Growing up, my family was very poor and couldn't afford a lot during the holidays. The evening of Thanksgiving, someone rang our doorbell and had left a full Thanksgiving dinner at our doorstep. —*Jeena E.*

Dress for the Occasion

ELISSA M.

When you're a teenager without a steady income stream or a family with the means and willingness to bankroll your social life, you have two choices: You can either find a way to do things cheaply, or not do them at all.

I chose to do things cheaply, which is why I found myself shopping at Goodwill for a winter formal dress. I'd scrounged together a grand total of $40 to pay for the outfit plus accessories; my family and I were temporarily living in a motel at the time, so there was no way I could ask my parents for extra money when they were already struggling to pay the bills. But there was also no way I was going to sit in that tiny room while my friends danced the night away without me.

The racks that day were full of options, ranging in appearance and quality on a scale from things my grandmother would (and probably did!) wear all the way down to something that looked like it was found behind a dumpster. But in the middle of the formal wear rack, I found it: a beautiful, frothy pink ballet gown with a sparkly neckline. The price tag read $39.99—within my budget, if I borrowed shoes and a necklace and used the five-dollar bill I always kept hidden for emergencies in the side pocket of my purse.

I held it up, considering. The size looked right, but I needed to make sure. I carried the dress to a fitting room, closed the curtain behind me, and tried it on. Holy crap, I looked amazing. The dress didn't look like it had ever been worn, and it fit me perfectly. I turned round and round in the mirror, looking for tears or snags in the fabric, and couldn't believe my luck when I didn't find one thing wrong with it.

Standing in line to check out, I bit my lower lip to keep from grinning like a lunatic. When it was finally my turn, I carefully passed the dress to the woman behind the counter and pulled out my wallet.

"Your total is $53.48."

My mouth fell open.

"What?"

She repeated the total, this time more loudly.

I stammered a bit. "But … the price tag says $39.99. Plus 7 percent sales tax. That should come to about $42."

She picked up the tag and squinted, before typing some numbers into the computer. "This price isn't right. It should be $49.99. All those fancy dresses back there are the same price. Not sure who put this sticker on it, but it's wrong."

Was she looking at me accusingly? I could feel blood rushing to my face and my hands getting hot as I shifted my feet.

"I only have $45 in my purse. Can you hold this for me while I run home and get a few more dollars?"

Not sure where I was going to find those dollars, I was determined to get them somehow. "No, we don't hold anything for anyone here. *Next customer, please!*" she barked. I swallowed hard, weighing my options before deciding that the best thing to do would be to hide the dress away in the back of the store, then rush home and locate more money.

As I turned around to look for a good hiding place, I felt a hand on my arm.

"Wait, honey. I'm buying this dress for you."

A pair of kind, brown eyes looked at me from beneath a Lakers baseball cap. The hand on my arm belonged to a woman who was behind me in line, watching the entire exchange. I felt tears prick at the back of my eyes as I whispered, "Why won't they just hold it for me? This dress is so perfect for the dance, and I almost have all the money." The woman threw a look of disdain at the cashier, who was now pointedly ignoring both of us. "Add this young lady's dress to my items, please," she said, before turning back to me.

I was busy pulling my cash out again to hand it to her, but she emphatically shook her head.

"No. You use that money to buy yourself some beautiful accessories. And please, enjoy yourself! I remember how exciting it can be to get all dressed up."

Sometimes, when I see groups of girls out at dinner during prom season, I think about the way I felt on the night I wore my pink ballet gown. I looked just as beautiful as everyone else, and I felt absolutely unstoppable.

What a gift to give a total stranger! I don't know what inspired that woman to help me out, but her act of kindness reminded me that people can actually be pretty awesome. ∎

Pay It Forward

HARRIET L.

It was December 2000. Days after moving from Florida to Albany, New York, my husband and I were traveling to northern Westchester for a family function. A dressy family function.

When we left Albany, it was raining. As we drove south, the rain began to turn into snow, and the roads were suddenly very slick. That was the moment a crazy person in a 4×4 pulled out, passed us, cut back into our lane, and then brake-checked us hard.

Well, his rugged winter 4×4 tires had no problem. But remember how we'd just moved from Florida? Our tires didn't hold the road … at all. To my husband's credit, he somehow managed to keep us from hitting anything solid. But eventually, our luck ran out and we ended up in a three-foot snowdrift on the side of the road. The car did a complete 180 on its way off the road and we were now facing north.

We surveyed the damage. Miraculously, there was none, except we were stuck in a snowdrift, pointed in the wrong direction, while wearing dress clothes.

Just then, a guy pulled up behind us and asked if we needed help. We admitted that we did. He said, "Get back in your car, stay warm, and I'll be right back with a shovel."

So we did. Just as we started wondering if he actually was going to come back or was playing a cruel joke on us, he pulled up.

Out pops the original guy, along with three of his friends and four shovels. They'd brought a bunch of road flares—useful, as we were parked by a curve and it was still snowing. In what felt like no time at all, they'd dug us out. Then, they (and my husband) pushed the car along the lane until we found a safe place to turn around.

When we asked if we could do anything to repay them, they declined. They just said, "Pay it forward." Those words—that request—are exactly why there's a tow strap in the back of my Jeep now. ∎

SPOTLIGHT

A staff member at a railway station drove me to the next town, as the train had broken down. I was on the way to see my nan; I had no idea that was to be the last time I ever saw her alive. That stranger has no idea just how much her kindness meant to me. —*Jodie B.*

Hug It Out

ANNA B.

My limbs hold a deep ache, like someone has their hands around them, squeezing as hard as they can. I have a fever: My head pounds and my body sweats bullets. I am profoundly tired. It feels like thousands of bricks are piled on top of me, pinning my body to the bed. The worst part? It's not unusual.

I have myalgic encephalomyelitis/chronic fatigue syndrome (ME/CFS). As a 19-year-old, I contracted Epstein-Barr virus, and then got mononucleosis. Shortly after, I developed ME/CFS.

> Although classified as a neurological disorder by the World Health Organization, chronic fatigue syndrome is an invisible, multisystemic chronic illness that is overwhelmingly ridiculed and disbelieved.

Although classified as a neurological disorder by the World Health Organization, chronic fatigue syndrome is an invisible, multisystemic chronic illness that is overwhelmingly ridiculed and disbelieved. The very name of the disease makes it mocked. "Just drink some coffee!" I'm often told. And "You don't know what tired is until you're a mother!"

Having this condition strained my relationships immensely. Most of my friends, like the rest of the world, thought I was making it all up. They were convinced I canceled plans because I was dodgy; I explained that I could barely move my body, but my explanations were to no avail. I guess they weren't really friends. But, still, I was so sad, full to the brim with shame and guilt.

One day, I walked down to my pharmacy, my legs aching and my head spinning, to pick up some medicine. A new pharmacist was working. She was short and wearing a clean, white lab coat.

When she called my name, I stood up and walked toward her. As she reached across the counter to hand me the prescription, she remarked that she'd never heard of this medicine before. I explained that it was new, an experimental medication for ME/CFS. I rattled off the acronym for my condition without thinking, and then braced myself for the inevitable explanation that always followed.

"For what?" she asked, her eyebrows furrowing.

"ME/CFS. Chronic fatigue syndrome."

"What's it like?" she asked.

"Uh …" I was surprised she was asking, but I decided to be honest. "It's awful. At my worst I'm bedridden; at my best I can take a short walk. I'm in constant pain. My body always hurts. It's like having the flu but every day of your life. Plus I can't sleep and I can't think. I'm always freezing cold or boiling hot. Light and sound give me a migraine. Only 10 percent of us get better. There's no cure. And research for it is underfunded because it's an invisible illness."

She nodded her head as I spoke. When I finished, I prepared myself for the usual, dismissive response.

"Wow," she said. "ME/CFS, you said, right?"

"Yes," I replied.

She scribbled on a piece of paper and told me that she was writing it down to research later. I cocked my head in surprise. Nobody, and I mean nobody, had ever taken the time to learn about my condition, and I wasn't quite sure how to react. As I considered this, she asked if she could give me a hug.

My eyes widened as I nodded yes. She came around the desk and embraced me.

"I'm so sorry," she said quietly. She held me in the hug, and tears welled in my eyes.

"Thank you," I whispered.

I didn't know there were people out there like her. This kind woman showed me that if people wanted to learn about what's really going on with someone, they would—which, in turn, meant that it wasn't my job to justify my existence. This was a relief. I'd spent so long trying to get people to understand me; I'd begged for acceptance more times than I can count. But after my interaction with the pharmacist, I stopped.

There are more people like her in the world—people who are understanding and caring—and those are the people I want to be around. I've even learned to stop villainizing those who diminish my experience. A lot of people can only relate to something they've experienced personally. But every once in a while, you find someone who wants to understand, even if they've never been there themselves. That's what empathy is, and that can make all the difference in the world. ▪

SPOTLIGHT

I moved to New York after college with only two oversize, wheelless suitcases to my name. It was my first adult move, into an apartment I had seen only once, with a woman I didn't know. By the time I realized the cab had dropped me off at the wrong address, the driver was already halfway down the block.

A group of older women on their stoop saw me on the curb, looking lost, and asked where I was going. When I explained, one grabbed her folding shopping cart, while the others took either end of my second suitcase to help lighten the load. And while the new place was only a block away, I'll never forget how their warm, simple gesture instantly made me feel at home in a city I was told would be so hard and cold. —*Modesta Z.*

Mojo and Daisy

CHRISTINA M.

Mojo and Daisy entered my life when I was 29 years old, living in my father's house without air-conditioning. I was working at a Subway in a truck stop, trying to improve my credit so I could move into a place of my own. It was an unbearably hot summer, and I was truly just trying to get by.

Now that I've set the scene, allow me to introduce Mojo Gonzales, my first Chihuahua. He looked like a little rat: small, brown, and very cute. Mojo was a mama's boy. He only went outside if I let him, enjoyed food from anyone he could convince to give him a scrap, and preferred my cuddles to everyone else's.

A few months after getting Mojo, I got him a girlfriend: Daisy May Sunshine. Daisy was a tan-and-black Chihuahua with an all-white belly and little pink ears. Daisy, however, refused to breed with Mojo. So, instead of lovers, they became friends.

Mojo loved Daisy. Whenever Daisy rested blissfully on my couch, Mojo jumped up next to her and licked the insides of her ears. After tolerating this for a few minutes, Daisy would growl softly at him, her teeth showing ever so slightly. Daisy was peaceful and Mojo was full of energy. They balanced each other perfectly, and were wonderful companions to me.

Because of our lack of air-conditioning, I never minded working my shifts at the sandwich shop—it was a relief, honestly. One day, an older woman entered the store and placed an order. I spread condiments on a white roll, then piled on sliced meat. We chatted idly about the oppressive heat wave, and I found myself telling her that my house wasn't air-conditioned.

"Oh, that's so awful. I have to have AC in my house because I have dogs," she replied.

My heart dropped. I felt so guilty about them already. I kept all the fans on and the windows open. I left out bowls of ice water and froze little veggie snacks for them.

I nervously told her that I understood, because I felt guilty every day for leaving my two buddies at home to sweat it out in the heat. She could probably sense my shame and disappointment; I felt like a horrible pet owner. She assured me that I was doing my best, that the dogs would be fine. But I couldn't shake the guilt as I bagged up her order.

A week later, the woman came back and ordered another sandwich. She asked me about Mojo and Daisy, and after I completed her order, she asked me to step outside.

"I have something for you," she said. "Come with me! It'll be real quick!"

"Ha, what?" I asked, uneasy.

"Just come outside for two seconds!"

Nobody else was in the Subway, so I stepped outside. She walked quickly in front of me and opened the trunk of her car.

"For you! You can have it for free," she said, pointing to a portable air conditioner nestled in the back. My eyes widened, and I installed it that night.

Every time I punch that thing on, I marvel that a total stranger gifted me an air conditioner with no expectation of anything in return. She just wanted my dogs to be happy. Her random act of kindness was a gift in itself, reminding me that there are good people in the world—people who do kind things for other people (and two little Chihuahuas) just because they can.

After so much evidence to the contrary—and as a food service worker, I could tell you stories—this remarkable woman is a breath of fresh (and air-conditioned) air. ■

Drumroll...

ROBERT B.

My first job out of college was at Guitar Center, which is a great place for an aspiring musician to work as long as he's got a lot of money to spend on all the badass equipment. But if I had a lot of money to spend, I wouldn't have been working in retail. So you see the conundrum here.

It was the holidays, which is a particularly crazy time to be in retail. Tons of people, tons of transactions, and not a whole lot of appreciation. I'd dealt with a lot of pretty terrible customers, and it was Christmas Eve. I was so ready to clock out and go home!

A man approached me for help with drumsticks, and I noticed right away that he was polite. What a relief! It turns out, he was a drummer like I was, and he was looking for some guidance on what pair of sticks to get. I talked to him about a particular pair I wanted, and how they were really great. He seemed to take my enthusiasm to heart, because he picked not one but two pairs of sticks off the shelf.

Imagine my surprise when I rang him up at the cash register and he gave one of the pairs to me. I couldn't believe it—it almost brought me to tears on the spot. I'd always known there was a certain type of brotherhood/sisterhood with drummers, but this just proved it to me beyond a shadow of a doubt. For this guy to help out a fellow drummer really meant the world to me. It helped restore my faith that most people are good, most people care, and on occasion they recognize an opportunity to make a big difference with a seemingly small gesture.

Now, I carry this anonymous drummer's kindness with me, always looking for the opportunity to make someone else's day. Because kindness, really, can come from anywhere. It can even be as simple as buying a pair of drumsticks. ∎

Nothing Lasts Forever

ALEAH B.

About seven years ago, I worked as a dental assistant. I loved my job, but wanted more—namely, to become a hygienist, which required going back to school. I've never been what you might call academically inclined; school just wasn't my thing.

But my main obstacle wasn't learning. It was test taking that never failed to cripple me with anxiety. Something about the ticking clock, the phrase "true or false," little rows of bubbles, the quiet—yeah. Instant cardiac event. I was like a drowning person whose panic ensured her doom. Which is to say, I never knew if I was actually out of my depth, or if fear just made it feel that way.

Still, with my family's support, I went ahead and took the plunge, registering to take the placement test required to enroll. Maybe it'll be OK, I thought. It wasn't. I showed up and did my best, but my anxiety did me one better, ensuring that I bombed. I was crushed, but not surprised. One thing I can say about test anxiety: It's reliable.

So, after the mauling, I went to the mall—because disappointment demands calories. As I sat alone in the food court, it really hit me: I had failed. To achieve my dreams, I'd either have to confront that test again—the mere thought of which made me sweat—or resign myself to taking a bunch of mind-numbing remedial classes. The first option tested my nerve; the second option tested my sanity.

Overcome with fear and powerlessness, I did what any self-respecting aspiring dental hygienist would do and cried uncontrollably into my lunch. Makeup ran down my face. People stared. I didn't care. I was locked in place.

A few minutes into this meltdown, a man in his late 30s approached my table. "Are you OK?" he asked. I couldn't speak because I was crying so hard, so he asked if he could sit. I nodded yes, and he handed me a fistful of napkins. As I attempted to steady my breathing, he sat there quietly, waiting for me to calm down. At last, my tears slowed, and then he said something that would become a personal mantra for life: I don't know what you're going through, but it won't last forever.

With that, he gave me a hug and walked away. I never saw him again.

That day proved to be pivotal because it was when I realized that nothing—not even fear—lasts forever. As time passed, I kept whispering that phrase—over and over—to myself, which eventually gave me the push I needed to dive back into school. I pursued my dreams with that motto in mind: every test, every class.

> That day proved to be pivotal because it was when I realized that nothing—not even fear—lasts forever.

I ended up on the dean's list while finishing my prerequisite courses. And though dental hygiene school is very competitive, I found myself on the dean's list there, too. I proved everyone and myself wrong by graduating cum laude in 2021—something I never imagined was possible.

I love my work as a dental hygienist, just as I suspected I would. And, through even my toughest days and grouchiest patients, I adhere to the wisdom of the Mall Man's motto: Nothing difficult lasts forever. ∎

SPOTLIGHT

In 2019, my partner and I were driving to a wedding in a remote mountain town in California. Because Google Maps didn't account for major road closures caused by heavy rainfall, we ended up off-roading in a Toyota Corolla. We got stuck on a dirt road in a remote area for six hours without food or water, and we had barely any cell service and a dead car battery. As daylight faded, we started panicking and frantically shouting at the top of our lungs for help.

Miraculously, a family in a house several miles away heard us and came to our rescue in a dune buggy. They ended up feeding us dinner, letting us shower and spend the night in their guesthouse, and making us breakfast in the morning. They also replaced the car battery and towed the car all the way back to the paved road. They were a godsend after dealing with all the stress and fear of the day. —*Juliana D.*

Lunch Break

TONY A.

When I was 19 years old, an airport janitor set my life on a course for kindness.

I was at the beginning of basic training for my Army career. I had a long weekend off, so I made plans to fly back home. The closest airport was in Atlanta, which made me nervous; I was a small-town kid barely out of high school, and I was worried about getting lost. So as soon as my final class ended, even though it was late at night, I drove straight there without stopping. I didn't want to risk missing my early morning flight if I overslept.

My first mistake was skipping dinner on base. My second mistake was assuming that the Atlanta airport would have vending machines or shops where I could buy myself something to eat. I was starving, exhausted, carrying a duffel bag, and wandering aimlessly.

I approached a much older gentleman who was working as a janitor and asked him if there were any vending machines or small shops open where I could grab something to eat. There weren't. I took a deep breath, thanked him, and found a quiet place to sit. I propped my feet up on my bag, pulled my hat down low over my buzz cut, and distracted myself with thoughts of home. Being hungry and uncomfortable was part of my training, after all.

Half an hour later, I felt a tap on my shoulder. The janitor was standing in front of me, holding a lunch box. He cleared his throat.

"Hello, son. Here's my lunch. You can eat whatever you want out of it. I don't need it, but you sure look like you do!"

At first, I refused, but he wouldn't take no for an answer. I offered him some money and he refused that, too. I gratefully ate the sandwich and apple he'd offered. Later on, I tried to find him to thank him again for his generosity, but he was gone.

I'm 46 now, and over the years, I've made it a habit to keep an eye out for lonely diners sitting in silence or folks who are clearly bearing the weight of the world on their shoulders. It could be an elderly gentleman eating alone at a restaurant he used to frequent with a long-lost loved one or a middle-aged woman with a look of grief and concern over some terrible news she just received. You never really know.

My big takeaway from that janitor so many years ago? A small act of kindness can lift someone's spirits in unimaginable ways. I'll continue to pass it along at every chance I get. ∎

The Man
at the Desk

ANITA H.

M y friends and I are practically floating back from Madison
Square Garden to our hostel on 42nd Street. It's our first
time in New York—we're all 17 and 18 years old—and fresh off a
flight from England to see Michael Jackson in concert.

If ever there's a reason to cross the Atlantic, this is it: Michael Jackson in all his glittering glory. Arms linked, we howl "The Way You Make Me Feel" into the night sky, intermittently drowned out by the rush of the subway. Displaced air puffs up through metal grates, sending petal-size flecks of trash skittering down the sidewalk.

It's September 10, 2001. We've been here for six days and will be leaving in two. The plan is to wake up extra early the following morning, meet in the financial district at about half past eight, and check out the twin towers. But the concert goes late—we don't get to bed until 3 a.m.—and (surprise!) oversleep.

Well, all except my friend Kat. Our hostel—the Aladdin—is in a quite tall building, so rather than wake us, she creeps from her bed to go check out the roof. Clutching a cup of tea, she takes in the view: the gigantic signs and intricate patterns of light, the shifting traffic jigsaw, the infinite scroll of dot-size humans. Then, in the distance, a massive cloud of dust rises from the ground. Moments later: sirens.

She comes downstairs to shake us awake. Bleary-eyed, with throats raw from last night's revelry and with concert bracelets clinging to our wrists, we watch in real time as history plays out on TV—a tiny screen bursting oranges and grays. People around me are crying. I remember thinking: This isn't happening. This is a movie.

Outside, sirens keep coming, every diminishing wail overwhelmed by the next in line: an endless pulsation of sound. The bigger questions—about what this all means, about the ultimate human cost—have yet to hit me. I'm a kid in survival mode, consumed by my own predicament. How am I going to get home? How am I going to feed myself? How will I pay for the hostel? And then:

Oh my god. My parents.

When we last talked, I told them our plans for the day. For all they knew, I was there. Up there. I had to call them—but how? Like everyone else's, my mobile is useless; no one can get a signal. We're all just—stranded—clutching our phones like babies with fake keys.

I'm not sure how one moment connects to the other, but before I know it, I'm running around Times Square with Kat, pounding the pavement we'd floated across the night before, ducking in and out of various buildings. Some are abandoned—evacuated lobbies, empty escalators—while others have been transformed into hives of pure chaos. Hotel desks are swarmed.

Kat and I know we don't stand a chance, so we try some phone boxes, feeding coins into the black slot. But it's all useless; we don't even get a dial tone. Just those three wheedling notes—exclusive to landlines and public phones—playing the mean little melody that used to mean "no."

Finally, we enter a nearby building, jumping over the turnstiles. It's illegal, probably—we're definitely trespassing—but considering the context, we doubt anyone cares. We hoof it upstairs, peering in to all the different rooms. All are empty, except one.

Standing by a desk in an otherwise unpopulated office, a single, middle-aged man, impeccably dressed, speaks solemnly into a phone. He exudes a kind of authority, like a CEO or something—a captain going down with his ship. "Please," we say, rushing up to him, tripping over ourselves to explain. "Can we please-please-please use your phone?"

After hearing so many nos, we expect the same from him. Instead, without hesitation, he kindly hands us the receiver—this in a time when calls to England were astronomically expensive.

Kat calls first. Within seconds she and her dad are sobbing—just the relief of knowing she's OK. But when I call my parents, it doesn't go through. (Later, I'll find out they were on the phone with the British Embassy, desperately trying to get hold of me through the hostel.)

Eventually, it occurs to me to call a friend—an old friend from school I hadn't talked to in years. She promises to contact my parents, and I hang up the phone, vaguely reassured, but also numb. At least, the mission to call my parents provided something to focus on. Without it, I felt strangely untethered. I wish I could say I cried, but I didn't. Everything felt like a performance. Nothing felt real.

Now, more than 20 years later, I still think about the man at the desk, who, in the middle of a national disaster, delayed his journey home so two teenage girls could call their parents. Sometimes, I imagine I've seen him—I'll be walking down the street, when I'm struck by the sight of a man of a similar height and build with dark-rimmed glasses. I'll stare at him an extra beat, transposing the remembered person over the present one, seeing if they match up. But they never do. Even if they did, it wouldn't make sense. He's a much older man now—just as I'm no longer 18.

Every time I go back to New York, I try to find him, even though I have nothing to go on except his first name. Marty. The old hostel—the Aladdin, with its magic carpet views—isn't there anymore. The signs are all different. Pay phones don't exist.

All I have from that day is a plastic pen I snagged from the man's desk: blue and white, embossed with the name of his company. I once looked it up, only to discover that it, too, no longer exists.

I keep the pen in a box like some kind of relic: the finger of a saint. I'd never dare use it. But in my mind, I write endless letters—long, confessional tomes—to the man at the desk who I'll never see again, telling him how much his kindness meant to me. ∎

What I Remember Most

TERESA M.

W e were headed to a wedding anniversary party on Vancouver Island—just a fun little day trip to a farmer's field in late September. For the ferry ride over, I brought along my two-year-old daughter, her car seat, and a boyfriend with whom I'd just begun discussing marriage. We didn't say so out loud, but I think we both may have considered this trip a metaphor of sorts, connecting us from one life stage to another, from the Land of Maybe to the Island of Yes.

I don't remember, but I'm told it was a lovely day—the kind of joyful, sun-drenched time you cling to, refusing to let go. By the time we left, it was already dark, with a chill in the air. The car we took back to the ferry didn't have a seat belt in the middle seat, so we moved my daughter's car seat to the left. My boyfriend buckled up on the right, and I took the middle.

Riding around without a seat belt isn't something I'd normally do, but this was our last chance back to the ferry. Besides, it was a short ride, and I trusted our driver, who was half of the couple we'd come out to celebrate. But another driver in another car was hurtling through the dark at 60 miles an hour. I'd failed to consider him, far too content on my planet to scan the horizon for asteroids.

He was 19 years old, out delivering pizza. He treated that stop sign like a green flag on a racing course, speeding through the intersection, smashing into our sedan on the right side at 90 degrees.

The car flipped over headfirst, then tumbled sideways into a ditch, ejecting me from the back windshield. I landed on the hood of a passing car coming in the opposite direction. My feet smashed the windshield. Someone called 911, and the police arrived shortly thereafter.

Everyone else involved was injured, shaken, but very much alive. But when they saw me sprawled on the hood of the other car, less person than projectile, they presumed me dead. They felt for a pulse. Suspicions confirmed.

That could have been the end of my story. But it wasn't, thanks to an off-duty young hero named Tyler. He was also 19 years old, and he'd just finished his training as a volunteer firefighter. His fire station was at a nearby intersection, serving the remotely located homes in the area, and he just happened to be riding by on his bike: an amazing stroke of luck, because the accident happened on a secluded stretch of highway.

Tyler rushed over to my presumed-dead body. He took my pulse, waiting for a full 60 seconds before getting a beat. One of my lungs had been punctured, so my breathing was very shallow, likely adding to the strain on my heart. Next, he raced to the fire station and got a mask and oxygen to sustain me until the ambulance arrived.

I was rushed to the hospital and put on life support. My parents were called and warned I might not make it. The next 24 hours were crucial, they said. I was 24 years old.

The accident wiped that day—and many days before it—from my memory forever. But strangely, I do remember the coma: no senses firing, no light, nothing to see or feel or hear, just complete darkness. I was alone, but so aware—feeling myself in space as a sort of vector of infinite possibilities.

I understood I had been given a choice: I could either go back to living as I had been living—always on the go, prizing goals above grace, striving above being. Or I could choose a different path, embracing a life in which contentment isn't contingent on what I accomplished, but on whom I loved—including myself.

I wasn't done with this life, I realized. My daughter needed me, and I still had so much to learn. Waking from that coma was the first step of what would prove to be a lifelong journey of recovery.

It hasn't been easy, but it's been worth it. Life is a gift. In times of struggle, when my footing falters, I think about Tyler—a complete stranger—taking my pulse, refusing to let go when everyone else did. Of all the things I don't remember, that's the thing I remember most.

I live my life in gratitude to him. ∎

SPOTLIGHT

I ran out of gas on a lonesome stretch of desert highway with no cell reception. It was nighttime but still almost 100 degrees out. I had my dog with me and was quite worried about what would happen when the sun came up.

I managed to get to a campground that seemed abandoned at first, but I eventually heard the rumble of an ATV. I flagged down the driver and was nervous that he wouldn't be friendly. But after I explained my situation, he said, "So, you need gas? Well, we got plenty of that!" He gave me a couple gallons of his racing-grade fuel and I gave him all the firewood, cash, and whiskey I had left over from camping. He sent me on my way with the words, "That's why we're all here, to help each other out." —*Mark T.*

CHAPTER TWO

Learn by Heart

The most important lessons

Keep an Eye Out

GABRIEL R.

I t's my first day of school. Kindergarten: the Big Leagues. I've already been given an assignment to have ready the first day—memorizing my home phone number and address—and I'm determined to crush it.

My mom's behind the wheel of our old Volvo station wagon, and I'm in the back seat, repeating numbers in my (bowl cut–enhanced) head. On the vinyl upholstery, a seam filled with beach sand reminds me of summer—a simpler time before the pressures of kindergarten descended. It feels so long ago.

I enter the front door to the classroom and linger there for a second, taking in the scene—rows of desks, the heady smell of crayon shavings and paste. Kids my age mill about, turtle-like in their backpacks, calling dibs on cubbyholes, greeting each other at the reasonable volume of howler monkeys on fire. The kids are all a little blurry—and that's when it hits me. These kids have two working eyes. I only have one.

Most people know amblyopia as "lazy eye"—a term I don't love. My eye didn't drift because it lacked a strong work ethic. It drifted

because it was abandoned by the government—that is, my brain. Basically, my brain and eye experienced a failure to communicate, and my brain—unable to access crucial visual information from one eye—gave up and learned to depend on the other. As my stronger eye started to do all the work, my weaker eye just sort of checked out, disillusioned by the system.

There's an easy fix, however, assuming your eye muscles and optic connections are still developing: Cover the strong eye. With the strong eye out of commission, your brain no longer has a choice: It *has* to redirect and build a bond with the weaker eye. Eventually, the weak eye gets stronger, and though it may never wind up delivering perfect vision, it's a lot better than the alternative of no vision at all.

Instead of a cool pirate's patch, I found myself afflicted with a flesh-colored fried egg–shaped Band-Aid—parrot not included. I didn't care, though. I figured lots of kids had to cover their eyes with Band-Aids—that it was normal, like bringing your lunch to school. It wasn't until I saw my patch-free classmates that I realized I was different. It was hard to look at them, literally—these lucky little two-eyed blurs—so I retrained my attention on the teacher. She may have been two-eyed, but she was a grown-up—so at least her eyes weren't at eye level.

> Mrs. Bean is larger than life. She appears in my memory as I knew her then; if I crossed paths with her today, I imagine she would still loom over me, 20 feet tall.

My first impression: Mrs. Bean is larger than life. She appears in my memory as I knew her then; if I crossed paths with her today, I imagine she would still loom over me, 20 feet tall. A fitting image, come to think of it—she was both the Bean *and* the Giant—but a friendly one, with a relaxing energy that put anxious kids like me at ease. She was just … safe.

When the bell rang, she asked everyone to sit on the floor in a semicircle. I dropped into place, as close to her as possible, training my one eye on the floor. Were people going to make fun of me? Would I make any friends?

Maybe Mrs. Bean picked up on my anxiety, or maybe she'd been prepped by my parents, who'd apprised her of my patch, expressing concern I'd be teased. Whatever the case, the first thing she did was ask me to stand up in front of the class. Mortifying, right? In that moment, I wanted to conceal myself entirely with a full-body-size patch.

"This is Gabe," Mrs. Bean said. "His eye is on vacation. Any questions?"

My classmates shook their heads no.

And that was that. In an instant, every kid in class accepted her explanation. *My eye was on vacation.* The rest of me? Present. Ready to learn and make friends—just like everyone else. Her story even gave my eye a sort of baller status, like it had better things to do. While my left eye occupied itself with Berenstain Bears books, my right was *on vacation*—sunning itself on a yacht in the Maldives, trading bon mots over martinis with James Bond.

In any case, my first impression of Mrs. Bean had been correct. She was nice, and she had my back. Things were going to be OK. (Well, except for that time Susan G. tried to flush my sweater down the toilet—but I don't think that was eye-related.)

That first day of kindergarten taught me a few things. One, kids aren't necessarily programmed to pick on other kids because they're different. Sure, there's inevitable curiosity as to why someone may look (or talk or walk) differently—a curiosity that, if left unsatisfied, can easily curdle into bullying. Mrs. Bean showed me how a good-hearted adult can ensure that doesn't happen. She was so good at making kids feel like they had a lot in common. Even our idiosyncrasies weren't divisive, because, after all, we *all* had them. ∎

When Words Get in the Way

TENY C.

I was an incredibly shy teen who couldn't speak in front of class, no matter how much I tried or wanted to. Teachers called on me anyway, told me to buck up and do it. They couldn't understand the surge of fear and anxiety that would choke me in those moments, and for the weeks and days before any sort of presentation. If they called on me in class, my brain and mouth wouldn't connect; I couldn't make a sound come out of my mouth no matter how much I tried. It was torture.

So, I just stopped studying. I decided I'd rather be the girl who didn't know anything; that way, my teachers would just stop calling on me altogether. And it worked—no one questioned it. They just wrote me off as a slow, quiet teen, thankful that I didn't cause problems in class.

But then I found myself in Mr. Ashman's Latin class. He had these in-class weekly oral quizzes, which of course I couldn't pass. I thought it would be the same old story—he'd write me off, I'd pass with a C for written assignments, and move on to the next grade. Instead, he surprised me: He asked why I didn't ever know the answers, though I did fine on written tests. I couldn't answer him, but a friend did for me, "She can't talk. She's too scared."

Instead of reacting poorly or telling me I needed to become more assertive if I wanted to have any chance at succeeding in life, Mr. Ashman did something completely unexpected. He crouched down next to me and said softly, "Next time, come to my desk at the end of class and you can whisper the answers to me before the next class arrives. But I want you to at least try."

And that was it.

From that moment on, I received perfect marks on every one of his quizzes. All because this man took the time to understand me, someone who was just shy and doing her best to navigate high school. He didn't think I should be penalized because of an overwhelming fear; he just found an alternative that made it safe for me to speak out loud and earn a good grade.

Mr. Ashman knew that differences didn't make you worth any less. And perhaps the most important lesson he ever taught me was how a seemingly small gesture can profoundly change someone's life for the better. My grades improved. I fell in love with learning all over again. And for that, I'll be forever grateful to him. ∎

Poetry in Motion

KELLEY S.

Everyone wanted to be in Ms. Bennett's fourth-grade class. Her outer (and more important, inner) beauty—a sparkling showcase of humor, joy, and empathy—went unmatched.

I was an extremely well-behaved student: an accomplished learner, never struggled with new material. Kids like me—the quiet, "no trouble" kids—sometimes slip under the radar. As the last of five children, I was generously loved but often felt invisible. I was definitely in need of being seen.

And so, I started to write stories and poems to express myself. Ms. Bennett returned them to me with words in the margins like "Wonderful!" "Amazing!" or "Just divine!" Her fancy script, followed by several exclamation marks and happy faces, made her words seem all the more sincere. I read them again and again, and their power never diminished.

One morning, in a burst of courage, I left a poem on her desk. I made sure the handwriting was as perfect as possible, hoping to compensate for the strangeness of sharing something that wasn't, you know, an assignment. Yep. I was such a Goody Two-shoes rule follower that even leaving an unsolicited poem on Ms. Bennett's desk felt like a high act of rebellion.

To my relief, she didn't think it was weird. In fact, that poem

> One morning, in a burst of courage, I left a poem on her desk. I made sure the handwriting was as perfect as possible, hoping to compensate for the strangeness of sharing something that wasn't, you know, an assignment.

marked the beginning of a year of nearly daily, secret correspondence. I felt she deliberately chose to get up from her desk—to go to the closet, check the office phone, or return something to someone's cubby—to provide me the opportunity to surreptitiously drop a new poem on her blotter. She'd smile at me at some point in the day with a sweet "Thank you" type of look, and my chest would swell with pride.

On the last day of school, something magical happened. All of Ms. Bennett's students had lined up for a hug goodbye—to tell her how much we loved her. When I finished my hug and took a step backward, she reached into her gigantic, fancy tote bag and pulled out two black bound journals.

She told me to open them. On the front page, in her lovely handwriting, she'd written, "The Poems of Kelley Shields." My eyes filled with tears.

"Thank you so much, Ms. Bennett," I said. And she replied, "No, thank *you*—your poems were the best part of each day. Please, keep writing." And so, I did. ▪

SPOTLIGHT

Mrs. Stephens, my second-grade teacher at Holbrook Elementary in Concord, California, gave me strength and confidence when I was diagnosed that year with dyslexia. The school told my parents that college probably wasn't in my future. Mrs. Stephens looked me in the eyes and said, "Let's prove them wrong." Well, Mrs. Stephens, wherever you are, I'm a Harvard alumna. Thank you for believing in me. —*Jennifer C.*

The Writing on the Wall

IRIS N.

I was nine and just getting used to my new name—an English appellation I had chosen from a dictionary. It met my mother's two very sensible requirements: something I could spell and say independently.

We'd emigrated from Hong Kong to England in 1995, and my teachers were desperately trying to get my English up to speed. "I like cats" and "This is not my cat" were only going to get me so far in a British school. I had no idea what anyone was saying, and I was terribly troubled by the word "shit." How would I ask for a sheet of paper without swearing? I could not hear the difference between long and short vowels.

Learning support teachers would take me out of class and have me read aloud, teaching me to sound out letters and feeding me exercise after exercise until—along came Mrs. Fearon. She brought me Christmas crackers and fairy cakes, and I realized English wasn't just a language but a door to an entire culture. One day, as we were reading, she pointed at a pair of words and said, "This is a rhyme. Like 'Humpty Dumpty' is a rhyme."

"What's that, Miss?"

I remember the gentle surprise on her face. Such popular knowledge is often taken for granted, but I was the girl who'd never seen snow or tasted carrot cake. Now, Humpty Dumpty beckoned me into a world of poetry from his perch on a wall.

Until that moment, text was there to be memorized; vocabulary was there to be absorbed and regurgitated for tests. But here, on the couch in the staff room with Mrs. Fearon, the text had rhythm. The text sang. It came to life.

Other teachers wanted me to spell, to read, but Mrs. Fearon pushed me to write. At a time when I could only read stories like "The Three Little Pigs," she alone dared to ask for more. More stories, more verse. I found myself scribbling poems in every margin of my books, senseless rhymes and made-up words—it didn't matter. The words poured out of me in narrative, in comic strips, in every form possible. Mrs. Fearon taught me poems I had no right to understand with my limited English—most notably, "The Owl and the Pussy Cat" by Edward Lear, which I loved so much I memorized it whole.

When I left that school, Mrs. Fearon gave me a goodbye gift: *A Children's Book of Verse*. A gorgeous green hardback full of watercolor illustrations, it spoke to my love of writing and art. But it wasn't until I met Mrs. Fearon that I realized that love had a name. She dared to ask me for words at a time when I had no words, dared me not to be confined by my limitations but to grow beyond them. To her, I wasn't just a foreigner who didn't speak English, but a child with a passion for language whom she nurtured.

Because of her, I started to write. And I haven't stopped writing since. ▪

Comfort Food

MARY K.

In 1993, I was 15 years old. *Jurassic Park* was showing in theaters. Kids were wearing baggy jeans, flannel shirts, and Doc Martens; my two favorite bands were Alice in Chains and Pearl Jam.

Also, I was pregnant.

The father of the baby was my boyfriend, a guy I met when I was 12. He was my older brother's friend. He played baseball, and made me feel seen. With him, I felt like I fit in somewhere—finally.

The pregnancy was an accident, and we tried to keep it quiet until it became clear that my morning sickness was going to make that impossible. Every morning in biology class, the nausea would hit me like a Mack truck. My sweet boyfriend couldn't do much to help besides feed me, so he brought a peanut butter and jelly sandwich to school every morning. I sat in class with a sandwich in my lap, sneaking bites to keep from retching.

The irony of grappling with pregnancy hormones while in biology class was not lost on me.

Being pregnant at 15 was an isolating experience. While the rest of my classmates were partying on the weekends and doing normal teenage stuff, I was studying and preparing for motherhood. Once my belly started showing, some of the teachers stopped calling on me in class altogether. I felt judged by my peers, I felt judged by adults, and I desperately wanted to sink into the ugly linoleum beneath my desk and stay there.

One morning while I was sneaking bites of my sandwich,

> Once my belly started showing, some of the teachers stopped calling on me in class altogether. I felt judged by my peers, I felt judged by adults, and I desperately wanted to sink into the ugly linoleum beneath my desk and stay there.

Mr. Wilkerson, the biology teacher, sauntered over to my desk. I shoved the sandwich farther into my lap, thinking I was about to be reprimanded. Instead, he leaned down and whispered kindly into my ear, "You don't have to sneak. You can just eat—it's OK!"

In that moment, all the shame and exhaustion I'd carried over the weeks and months disappeared. The kindness and lack of judgment in his face literally changed my life. He gave me permission to be myself—no apologies, no shame. That's an amazing gift to give another human being.

I carried that baby to term and married my boyfriend (now my husband of 28 years!), and we raised our daughter to adulthood. She graduated with a master's degree and recently started a family of her own.

To this day, I look back on Mr. Wilkerson with gratitude. A sandwich provides one kind of nourishment; compassion provides another. And the latter, for me, meant everything. ∎

How's the Water Today?

LEXI G.

I received my death sentence at two years old, with 11 years to live if I was lucky. I took 36 pills crushed into food and drinks, hoping it would give me more time. A guinea pig for new treatments, I spent more time in the hospital than I did on the playground. I was too little to understand that my childhood deviated from the norm. If you'd asked me at that age, "Hey Lexi, what's it like to be sick?" I wouldn't have had an answer—sickness was all I'd ever known. It's like that joke about the fish. You ask the fish, "How's the water today?" The fish replies, "What's water?"

At four and a half, I lost my mother to the same virus I had—the same one she unknowingly gave me. Her death was a drop in the water in which I swam—a drop so charged and potent it changed the color of my world.

Shortly after this, I started kindergarten. When the harsh reality of my illness hit full force, she wasn't there to help me swim.

At school, during nap time, I wasn't given pillows or blankets, or allowed to sleep near the other kids. Staff laughed at me while I put my legs through my jacket sleeves to stay warm. In first grade, if I spit or bled, I was sent home. I had my own bathroom, and was relegated to the far corner of the classroom. You see, I wasn't just ill with a typical cold or flu; I was ill with an invisible virus everybody feared.

My first lesson in school was this: You, Lexi Gibson, are not a kid to be loved. You are something unknown, something to be feared.

Middle school was a nightmare; bullying was on the daily agenda. Most of the time, no one sat with me during meals; I'd say I felt invisible, but it was actually quite the opposite. I was the laughingstock of the school, routinely shoved back and forth between people, all of whom jeered while calling me names. Paper wads and pennies were thrown at me during class. The day I died inside had to be the afternoon I showed up to science class to find huge scrawled letters on the door:

Lexi has AIDS.

Usually when a person has a terminal illness, they're met with empathy and love. But my HIV diagnosis provoked ridicule and loathing.

In seventh grade, though, I got lucky: Mrs. Marks was my science teacher. She was the only person in the whole school to treat me like a normal human being. She was the oxygen to my water, and didn't allow anyone to bully me under her watch. Funny and bright, she wasn't charismatic in a showy way, like a teacher in a movie who stands on a desk. She was grounded and empathic. She was real.

So, one day, at lunch, instead of signing up for another round of human target practice, I walked into her classroom and asked, "Could I eat with you?" She said, "Sure"—like a person who'd actually enjoy my company. After that day, her classroom became my safe haven. I don't think we talked about it, the bullying. But I knew she knew. She was one of those people, capable of unspoken understanding.

> I don't think we talked about it, the bullying. But I knew she knew. She was one of those people, capable of unspoken understanding.

Nothing momentous happened in that classroom; that's what made it special. Mrs. Marks and I would sit and talk, or watch movies, listen to music. Sometimes I'd draw or do homework. Sometimes we'd sit and be quiet, and it wasn't awkward; it was revelatory.

You see, in the water I swam in, chaos was the norm. At home, at school—people yelling, slamming doors, beating me, screaming insults. Even louder than that was the noise inside my head: the internalized mean girl on a loop. The one who told me without hesitation that I was worthless, a freak, unwanted, and impossible to love. I believed what everyone told me. But when I ate lunch with Mrs. Marks, for 50 minutes, the noise went away. For the first time since my mother died, I experienced something deeper than quiet. I experienced peace.

Abandoned by my father at 14, I found myself on my deathbed at 15, my organs shutting down. My adoptive mom (another story) fought hard to get me into a medical study with new medication that would "hopefully" save my life. I wasn't hopeful. I'd been in studies my whole life. Hope required energy I no longer had.

But I was wrong. This time, the drugs worked. My viral count dwindled until it virtually disappeared. Undetectable, they called it. I won't say it was a miracle and risk undermining the collective effort of thousands of scientists who dedicate their lives to making things like this possible. But I will say it felt like one.

I'm not going to lie. My problems didn't just go away; there's no drug you can take for that. A lifetime of being treated like an untouchable takes its toll. And it takes a truckload of therapy to convince yourself that you are not, in fact, a virus; you are a human worthy of love. Deserving of happiness, health, hope—all the *h* words that aren't "HIV."

At 31, I live in Las Vegas and own a beautiful ranch home on a half acre. I am surrounded by people who love and accept me— people like Mrs. Marks, who provided proof of kindness when I needed it most. The serenity I experienced in her classroom, once so rare, is now boundless. Drop by drop, I changed the water I swim in—from gloomy and turbulent to calm and clear. Love and belief are all I needed. After all, I know how precious life is; not a day goes by without gratitude to see another sunrise.

If you ask me now, "How's the water today?" This time, I have an answer. The water is beautiful. ∎

SPOTLIGHT

My mother. She's standing up for LGBTQ+ students in her district right now, despite her aversion to confrontation. I love her and am so lucky she's my mom. —*Caroline B.*

All the Beauty in the World

DAKOTA M.

As I watched neon green and hot pink lights dance through the Icelandic sky, I saw the wonder and magic of the universe on full display. And it made me think of Mr. O., my seventh-grade science teacher in Moore, Oklahoma.

Mr. O., a large Irishman with a peppered beard, always wore baseball caps and shirts with wild animals printed on them. He was a spectacular teacher, who always taught with our class pet, Bull the bull snake, resting on his shoulder. Mr. O. also opened an outdoor classroom, where we watched squirrels nibble on leaves, foliage change, and monarchs fly through the seasons. He reveled in bringing the wonders of nature to his students.

Mr. O.'s enthusiasm for teaching was palpable; he skipped as he taught, his voice inflecting as he explained scientific concepts. Mr. O. was not only a wonderful educator, but also a wonderful person. He was a support to his students, his door always open. Twelve-year-olds are prone to being mostly miserable, but Mr. O. made everything a little bit better.

Years ago in his classroom, I vividly remember him describing the northern lights. "When solar wind and Earth's magnetic field interact, these colorful lights swell up in the sky," he told us. His eyes widened, pointing enthusiastically to a photo of aurora borealis on the board. If they looked that cool in a picture, I could only imagine what they'd look like in person. But those lights were a long way away from Oklahoma.

I kept in touch with Mr. O. after seventh grade. And after I graduated college, my friend and I decided to take a trip to Iceland. She asked me what I wanted to do there. "I don't give a crap about doing anything besides seeing aurora borealis and texting a photo of it to Mr. O.," I replied to her.

And that I did.

"I can't believe you got to see all that! You fulfilled something I always wanted to fulfill!" he wrote.

Mr. O. taught me something that I always suspected was true—that there's a beautiful world out there, ready to explore. "You are the one who got me wanting to see it!" I replied. "Thank you." ▪

A Rose by Any Other Name

MARK H.

Brighton, Michigan, is a wonderful place to grow up. Slightly less wonderful if you're gay, but that applies to the whole world, I think, in the 1980s—a decade in which high school movie king John Hughes loomed large as the arbiter of teen dos and don'ts (for the record, being gay was a don't).

Brighton was exactly the kind of small, suburban town that Hughes could convince me I belonged in. I believed that, for the most part, until middle school, which proved to be a little slice of hell on wheels.

Without a doubt, hell on wheels—otherwise known as the bus—constituted the worst part of my childhood. The short distance from the entrance to my seat felt less like walking down an aisle than down a plank, with my torturers piled up in the back seats like gum-cracking, acne-prone pirates. Their weapon of choice: mockery. Their treasure: my winter cap, which they'd steal repeatedly with impunity, and—of course—my dignity.

> The funny thing is, at the time, I wasn't even sure what it meant, that word. But it didn't matter. Some words are delivered with such vehemence you can't help but understand their meaning.

Faced with bullying, my natural inclination was to draw back. But then it was like, Oh, you don't even fight back?! Another black mark against me. And sure, they loved calling me names—it's not like these twerps reinvented the wheel. They were particularly fond of the *f* word (the one with three letters, not four). The funny thing is, at the time, I wasn't even sure what it meant, that word. But it didn't matter. Some words are delivered with such vehemence you can't help but understand their meaning.

But, you know, I got through! In high school, I befriended the most popular girls in school, which shielded me from the worst of the bullying (no jock was about to risk alienating a girl for the paltry reward of humiliating her friend). Still, life at that time was more about defending myself than including myself—more about survival than self-discovery.

That is, until I met my English and drama teacher, Mrs. Diana Rose.

My first impression of Mrs. Rose was that she was awful. She was so strict: In her class, you didn't mess around—at all. She didn't exactly live up to her namesake: Diana, I associated mostly with an English princess, and Rose, with romantic flowers. But Mrs. Rose—with her grouchy face and buzzed hair, her thick eyeglasses—was pretty much the opposite. If she was at all roselike, it was because of her sharpness: Her direct and unequivocal feedback punctured our fragile egos like thorns.

But my feelings about her changed over time. I realized her strictness, though intimidating, ultimately drove our excellence. She wouldn't settle for less than what she knew we were capable of—and because of that, we discovered exactly how much that was: a lot, as it turned out.

After a while, as I got to know Mrs. Rose better, I realized her outward toughness masked a certain sensitivity. I first became aware of it when she assigned Oscar Wilde. Mrs. Rose could have easily taught the most superficial reading of his plays and his novel, *The Picture of Dorian Gray.* But instead, she chose a braver path and delved into the subtext, illuminating Wilde's impossible bind as both celebrated writer and persecuted gay man.

But my connection to Mrs. Rose was cemented later my senior year, during our long-awaited class trip to New York: the promised land. I'd never been to the city. But I'd tasted it, once, watching

Saturday Night Live. David Bowie performed—with Klaus Nomi, in total drag—and I'd never seen anything like it. It was a profound revelation: that there are these people out there—people John Hughes couldn't even begin to fathom. What is that world? I wanted to know. How do I access it?

Mrs. Rose, who served as our chaperone, opened the door. Even more impressive than the city, though, was my teacher herself. In New York, a whole other side of her appeared. Gone was the stern disciplinarian; in her place was a true rose. When she spoke to me about art and theater, music and dance, joy bloomed in her face. In that bright city, through those scintillating conversations, Mrs. Rose unwittingly demonstrated for me the power of authenticity: how being your true self—which she was in New York, free from classroom constraints—could make you beautiful. Could make you alive.

As soon as I graduated high school, I left Brighton and never looked back. ▪

SPOTLIGHT

Mrs. Resler, my fourth-grade teacher in Phoenix, Arizona. When we moved across town to a new school district with about a month left to go, she picked me up in the mornings and drove me across Phoenix so I could finish in her class. Forty years ago and I still remember our morning car rides together. —*Jeremy L.*

Speak Into the Universe

LAURIE S.

I believe that when we speak our truth, the universe listens.

I was six years old when I first dared to whisper out loud my dream of becoming a teacher. Life at home on the Yakama Indian Reservation in White Swan, Washington, was tough; my family was incredibly poor, and we lived without running water or electricity for many years. Our lack of hot water meant that baths happened only once a week, because the process of pumping water with a hand pump and then heating it up on the woodstove was long and arduous. People referred to my siblings and me as the "stinky Kanzleiters," and they were right. We really did stink.

By the time I was old enough to go to school, I'd already witnessed and experienced a lot of dysfunction. I was a shy, nervous child who struggled to speak up, and I felt like my fingernails were always dirty, no matter how hard I scrubbed at them. In stark contrast, the teachers at my school were clean, pretty, and, of course, smart. Their clothes were laundered, and they wore lipstick. They smiled with kind eyes, gave reassuring hugs, and instinctively knew how to help when I was struggling. I wanted to be like that.

> In sixth grade, I was assigned to Ms. Pastrana's class. She was younger than the other teachers, wore fashionable clothes, and, most notably, had brown skin like my own.

I wanted to be a teacher.

Going to school and learning—these were two things I could control despite the chaos at home, and it became my salvation.

In sixth grade, I was assigned to Ms. Pastrana's class. She was younger than the other teachers, wore fashionable clothes, and, most notably, had brown skin like my own. She was the first teacher of color I'd ever had, and she was so damn relatable. I looked forward to seeing her every day.

Unfortunately, my dedication to school wasn't enough to save me from my personal life. By age 14, I was homeless. I dropped out of school in the ninth grade and was pregnant at age 16. Two years later, I was pregnant again, and by the time I was 21 years old, I had three children.

My husband at the time was abusive and refused to allow me to go to college, but I managed to get my GED. For the next 20 years, I worked in warehouse jobs and focused on taking care of my family. I didn't completely forget about my desire to become an educator, though. It just got put on a shelf for a long time.

When I was 38 years old, still working in a warehouse doing heavy lifting, I became pregnant with my son, Tyler. The cost of day care made it clear that returning to my previous job wasn't an option; I wasn't earning enough to make it worth paying for childcare.

I'd always wanted to continue my studies beyond high school, so at age 40, I started looking into my options. I applied and was accepted to Green River College, where I attended two years before I was invited to apply to Antioch University's First Peoples' Education Program in Auburn.

One of my college assignments was to write a letter to a former teacher, so naturally I wrote to

Ms. Pastrana—and she wrote me back! I invited her to my college graduation—*and she actually came!* She drove all the way from Yakima to Seattle and was waiting for me when I emerged from the graduate staging room. I was wearing a cap and gown for the first time in my life, and my favorite teacher—the person who truly inspired me—was there to cheer me on.

I work hard every day to be as impactful of an educator for my students as Ms. Pastrana was for me. I now teach at a middle school and have the opportunity to empower children to speak their dream into the universe, just as I did so many years ago. ▪

Inventing the Future

SHAWN B.

When I was 12, my family moved from England to a small town in West Wales. I didn't speak a lick of Welsh initially, so not only did I get to be the new kid; I also got to be the new kid in a tight-knit bilingual school. Not the easiest.

The combo of not knowing anyone and not knowing the language made things feel pretty overwhelming, particularly when many lessons and interactions in school were in Welsh. Those early years, I spent a lot of time by myself—in nature, with my dog. (My dog didn't speak Welsh, either.)

On top of this, I am dyslexic. Most people associate this learning difference with difficulties around reading and writing—reversing letters and all that—but I rarely muddle letters. My dyslexia impacts my memory. Imagine a bridge connecting your short-term memory to your long-term memory, and everything you learn in school—facts, formulas, dates, quotations—crossing that bridge. For me, lots of things never make it to the other side of that bridge. As you can imagine, this made taking exams hugely challenging. My academic confidence took a big hit as a result.

However, there was something that couldn't be shaken: a love for making and inventing things. That's why I signed up for the Design & Technology class—because it was different from the rest. Meaning, it allowed for making and inventing things.

This class happened to be led by a teacher named Mr. Griffiths.

At first sight, Mr. Griff—as we learned to call him—was quite intimidating. He was a commanding figure, a gruff former rugby-playing Welshman (his name, in Welsh, literally means "strong grip lord") with a thunderous baritone. The moment someone dared to step out of line, Mr. Griff's voice dropped down like an anvil—BOOM!—keeping them in check.

But, as I got to know him, I realized he had a gentleness beneath that tough exterior. A closer look revealed an amused twinkle in his eye, even when he was angry or strict. If you showed him respect and enthusiasm, he responded in kind. Gradually, feelings of intimidation subsided; in their place grew trust and admiration.

By the time our A-level Design & Technology project came along, I'd plucked up the courage to approach Mr. Griff with a big idea: a custom vehicle fashioned entirely from sustainable or recycled materials—a solar-powered electric trike with the smallest carbon footprint possible. Rather than rein in my ambition, Mr. Griff helped break down the project into bite-size chunks. His encouragement made the impossible seem possible.

Without my knowledge, Mr. Griff entered my project into the U.K.'s National Engineering Competition. I was one of 150 semifinalists across the U.K. Barely had I gotten used to that idea when the judges narrowed it down to five finalists—including me.

Then, at a big glitzy award ceremony, roughly an hour after I threw up from eating bad takeaway, they announced that I had won. All thanks to Mr. Griff's faith in me—and a trike I created from bamboo and old bike parts.

I collected my award, hugged my dad, and took in the moment. But the highlight was calling Mr. Griff. He told me how proud he was, how he'd always known I had what it took to succeed—to win.

After I hung up the phone, I thought back to my very first impression of him: his scary demeanor and booming voice. But Mr. Griff not only saw my potential; he helped me realize it. He gave me the space to understand myself without judgment. For a time I thought of dyslexia as a curse, but now I know it gives me more strengths than challenges. It helps me see the world in a different way.

Because of this competition, I was able to go to a top university and study engineering. Even though I didn't have the grades, this competition allowed me to become an engineer. He quite literally changed the trajectory of my life. ∎

SPOTLIGHT

Mr. Owen, my 11th-grade ancient history teacher. He'd say things like, "So when you go to Italy, be sure to visit the …" Not *if* you have the odd chance of visiting Italy, but *when*. It made us feel like, yeah, why can't I go to Italy someday?!?! —*Julie R.*

Shine On

TIM F.

Once upon a time, a poster hung on the wall of a classroom that read, "Be the person you needed when you were younger." The owner of that sign, Mrs. Frost, was a humanities teacher at a local high school.

Mrs. Frost's own high school experience was so tough for her that she decided to keep a reminder for herself that kids deserve the freedom to be who and what they are. She's changed so many lives for the better—my own included—that I'm not quite sure where to begin.

I'll start with what I know: Mrs. Frost understood what behaviors were worth paying attention to. Kids who got in trouble with other teachers often thrived in her class because things like fidget spinners, doodling, and leaning back in their chairs were nonissues. She looked past the behavior in order to see the child, and they soaked up her positive energy like rays of sunshine.

Because Mrs. Frost knew what was worth paying attention to, she took an interest in her students outside of the classroom. One student, Kae, gave her a folder filled with poetry. Kae was a gifted writer, but some of their work included heavy themes of self-harm and other markers of depression. Mrs. Frost immediately recognized the red flags and alerted Kae's parents. After an emotional meeting, Kae got the professional help they needed and began to turn a corner. Kae said if it wasn't for Mrs. Frost's compassion, awareness, and quick action, it would have been the last day of their life, as they had been contemplating suicide.

Be the person you needed when you were younger. That's Mrs. Frost's motto, and she lives it every day: at home, at work, and in her relationships. I've seen it firsthand, because I'm her husband. (As I said, she knows what's worth paying attention to!) ▪

Meeting My Own Reflection

SANDY Y.

In the poem that brought Joe Saskatch into my life—a life I now credit him with saving—a girl walks down the street, alone, and turns a corner. And then, she runs into herself.

I wrote this thing, oh, 50 years ago? So, I don't remember the exact lines. I do remember the general feeling of the poem—deeply unhappy—and the way it ends: with the girl not liking the person she sees.

Joe was my English teacher at the time. He read the poem and must have recognized it as a cry for help, because next thing I know, I'm being pulled aside by the school psychologist: Would I like to come in and talk? Um. No thanks, lady. The whole point of writing poems was to avoid talking. There was no way I could speak this pain out loud—not to her, not to anyone.

I was adopted from Japan and brought to the United States when I was about 15 months old. Half Japanese, half white, and fully screwed, thanks to my new adoptive grandmother. It takes a special kind of person to hate a child, but she managed.

From the minute my parents left for work, she became ruler of the roost and, as such, focused on two priorities: (1) making sure her grandkids didn't die, and (2) finding ingenious ways to remind me I wasn't, in fact, her grandkid. I was, as she put it, "a sneaky little Jap," whose people, she'd remind me, started the war. If I dared to defend myself—if I mentioned, for example, that I couldn't be responsible for something that happened before I was born—I was swiftly punished. Rule number one in our household: Do not talk back to your elders. Even when they're cruel. Even when they read bedtime stories to your white siblings and force you to listen from outside, in the hall. Even when they cut your face out of family pictures.

By the time I was a teenager, despite all outward signs of resistance—yelling, tears, slammed doors—inside, I'd surrendered, internalizing her point of view. I wasn't a kid, right? I was a bomb, my grandmother's personal Pearl Harbor, dropped out of nowhere on her split-level home in suburban New Jersey, ruining everything. I didn't think of my anger back then as justified; rather, it was more proof that she was right and I was wrong. Is it any wonder then, that on rounding that corner in my poem and seeing myself for the first time, I hated who I saw?

Joe Saskatch was the first adult in my life to see something else. He was like that—with all the kids, not just me—and especially the kids who were hurting. His personal mission was to convince us we were more than we thought we were.

In addition to teaching English, he was also the high school drama coach. Not only did he inspire a passion for theater that stayed with us our entire lives, but he also subtly healed us through the plays we performed. For instance, in Chekhov's *The Seagull,* he cast me as Masha, a moody young woman dressed in black who famously opines: "I'm in mourning for my life." Poor Masha—so depressed, so rejected. But, playing her, I didn't judge her—I developed compassion instead. For her. And myself.

My senior year, we did *Antigone*. Joe cast me as Ismene, the "fair and beautiful" younger sister to Antigone's fierce, less fair-forward older sister. Unfortunately, Antigone was played by the prettiest girl in our class: blond hair, blue eyes—everyone was in love with her. I was so self-conscious as Ismene—introduced again and again as the "fair and beautiful" Ismene in the presence of this girl. Finally, I brought it up to Joe. No one was going to buy me as "the pretty one," I insisted—not when I'm standing onstage next to this goddess.

It had yet to dawn on me that my self-perception wasn't a universal truth—that my self-image had perhaps been warped by a grandmother who shamed me for my looks. I credit Joe with planting that first seed of awareness—for casting me in a role that pushed me to consider, for the first time in my life, that maybe she was wrong.

Once, he said to me, "Sandy, you are better than the bad things going on around you." I didn't quite get what he meant at first. But eventually the message hit home. I wasn't hideous—not on the outside, and not on the inside, either.

Thanks to Joe, I not only worked up the confidence to play Ismene, but to go on and pursue a career in theater. Even though everyone in my family told me, "Don't. You'll never get parts. You'll never get a job because of the way you look."

But it was too late—I didn't see myself as they saw me anymore. I saw myself through my teacher's eyes: a good person; an artist worthy of pursuing her dreams; a young woman who, upon rounding the corner and meeting herself, didn't have to hate the person she saw. I saw myself through my own eyes—no longer an enemy, but a friend.

Joe died a long time ago, but he's still with me as a presence. One good friend said the same thing of him not too long ago: Every now and then when he's feeling down, he remembers how much time and energy Joe put into each one of us—the wounded ones, the outsiders he took under his wing. So now, when I feel that maybe I'm not as good as I should be, I hear his voice inside my head: You're more than you think you are. ∎

SPOTLIGHT

Ms. Schreiber, my third-grade elementary school teacher. She loved me and would always hug me every day, noticing my strengths and complimenting me. It really helped because I was a sensitive girl; my head was always in a book. I eventually returned to Korea, grew up, and became an English teacher. I wish I had reached out to let her know. She would have been so proud. —*Cindy P.*

Of Course I Will

NIX H.

In high school Spanish, we weren't taught the singular "they." It was always "he or she," *él* or *ella*. For most of my life, I identified with she/her pronouns, but during my senior year of high school, I began to feel more connected to they/them. I was just too scared to tell anyone—it didn't feel safe. I still haven't told my parents because they wouldn't accept it.

But then, during my first semester of college, my Spanish professor mentioned that one of her children, Georgie, sometimes uses they/them pronouns. She assured us that, should we ever choose to use the pronouns of our choosing, she'd do her best to adjust accordingly.

Still, I kept my pronouns to myself. Two-thirds of the way into the semester, however, my professor and I started emailing, because I was struggling to catch up in class. Sometimes, I told her, I found it difficult to focus, because I'd be seized by sudden, inexplicable panic attacks. "Thank you for letting me know," she emailed back. "I'm so sorry that happened."

Remembering what she said about pronouns, I replied, "If you wouldn't mind, could you use they/them with me instead of she/her?"

My heart pounded, anticipating her reply.

"Of course I will," she replied. "And if I ever forget in the future, please remind me."

Reading her words, I felt so loved and validated—finally, I'd met an adult with whom I felt safe enough to share my pronouns. Because my Spanish professor was the first adult I told, she set the tone for how it would feel to reveal myself to the world. Her warm and understanding response made the future seem much less daunting. ∎

Opening Story

BELINDA M.

Mrs. Lester was my fourth-grade teacher when I was nine years old. She had a touch of genius in her for sure. I always thought that if she lived in another time or place, she would have become a famous writer on Broadway.

She once wrote a completely original musical about an aardvark and an army of ants, and another about King Arthur and his band of knights. One day, I recall her climbing out of our classroom window with an invisible number line in her hand, to demonstrate to us the concept of infinity. "Think farther than this classroom," she called out to us from the lawn. "Think farther than this school. Think of a vastness humans can't even begin to comprehend."

She burst with creativity, that woman, and it lit some sort of fire in me. Mrs. Lester didn't live in a big glittering city—she lived in the same place I did: a tiny village in a country on the tip of Africa. I'm so grateful we found ourselves in each other's worlds, because at the end of each day—once we'd finished our sums and spelling, once we'd started to get a bit tired—she'd sit us down on a mat at the foot of her striped, green armchair and read us a story.

What I remember most is our rapt silence. Nobody acted out or became distracted, because she read with such intensity. We hung on every word. My favorite book she chose was *Charlotte's Web*. Through Mrs. Lester, the characters came alive, leaping from the pages to snort and cluck and dance—and, of course, write glistening messages in spider silk. I fell in love with the power of stories then and there: from their ability to transport us to other worlds and to make us think, feel— even redirect our lives. But, of course, more than the story pulled me in. It was also Mrs. Lester's compelling performance.

Today, I'm a writer. It's possible I'd have chosen this path without Charlotte's inspiring messages. But without Mrs. Lester? Not a chance. ∎

Of Deer and Donkeys

DeANDA F.

I will never forget a truly awkward day in Latin class when I confidently stated—in my loudest, most animated voice: "The tiny donkey slipped around in the honey on the table."

The class giggled—a sure sign I'd translated the ancient poem incorrectly. I flushed; my forehead prickled with beads of sweat. I was mortified—like a tiny donkey who slipped in honey in front of all the other smarter donkeys. I stared at the floor, unable to face the inimitable Dr. Streufert, a teacher we all respected and admired.

I had already felt out of my league as an older student transferring into a new program. I lacked foreign language credits, and due to my late registration, all that remained open was Latin. So, there I was with my bright red face, surrounded by snickering classmates who all knew the correct translation was much less comical than what I had proposed.

Dr. Streufert, I noticed, was laughing, too—but in a different way than my classmates. His amusement was more understanding in nature. When he jokingly assured me that my version of the poem was a lot more entertaining than the original, I relaxed a little. And when he shared with the class that he, too, had made similar gaffes, I felt exonerated. Apparently, he'd once translated "a deer living outside the city walls" as "the deer vomited outside the city walls."

It wasn't just me, I realized—ancient languages can be tricky. Dr. Streufert wanted us to know that these things happen, and that this was a safe space.

Dr. Streufert made such a lasting impact on me that I followed in his footsteps and became an ancient world humanities teacher. Now, if a student makes an error in front of their peers, which invariably happens, I share the tale of Dr. Streufert and the donkey. Mistakes, I reassure them, are nothing to be ashamed of. Mistakes are how we learn. Mistakes are what help us grow. ▪

How Does This Movie End?

CAITLIN M.

Sophomore year of high school was, by far, my hardest. I was horribly anxious and started to struggle in school. Whether my difficulties stemmed from my anxiety or my anxiety stemmed from my difficulties is hard to say. All I knew was that I'd gone from tasting the sweet honey of straight A's my whole life to being swarmed by B's. To an anxiety-afflicted person navigating high levels of perfectionism, B's were basically F's. *Unacceptable,* bellowed the relentless drill sergeant in my head. *Do better.*

Some people made my anxiety infinitely worse; a science teacher publicly shaming students who asked questions comes to mind. But my algebra teacher—let's call him Mr. C.—was different. Like in that parable about giving someone a fish to eat versus teaching them how to fish, he not only eased my anxiety, but also gave me the tools to tackle it myself.

Mr. C. was one of those teachers you never forget: a witty and all-around brilliant man who cared deeply about his students. Algebra was really confusing for me, and I would come to him nearly every day for extra help, panicked about failing the next quiz, test, or homework assignment. That my dire predictions never materialized did nothing to prevent my conviction that this time would be different. As I fretted at his desk, plagued by visions of doom, Mr. C. looked at me with calm equanimity.

"Caitlin," he'd say with a reassuring smile. "How does this movie usually end?"

For whatever reason, the question never failed to ground me. Like, wait a minute: I *did* know how this movie ended, and it wasn't going to be with an asteroid hitting Earth. The movie ended with palpable relief—a good grade—and a teacher who consistently met my anxiety with compassion and strength.

Years later, as a student at the University of Michigan, I was sometimes overwhelmed by the rigorous demands of college academics. But I would remember Mr. C. and pose his question: How does this movie end?

Well, it ended with a 3.8 GPA. And the realization that, ultimately, grades don't matter; it's the story we tell ourselves that counts. Unlike movies in the theater, the movies we create every day are less about plot than they are about character.

At the very end of my film—starring me, co-starring my anxiety—the credits will read:

Special thanks to Mr. C. for making all this possible. ▪

Reading Out Loud

SARA C.

Reading out loud in class is literal hell for a kid with dyslexia. Whenever I had to read something, I would shield my face with my hands to hide the bright red embarrassment underneath. Some kids have a gift for sensing weakness in others, so I got made fun of. A lot.

In sixth grade, I had a new teacher: a huge bear of a man with a heart of gold named Mr. Cook. He was a legend in our little town—a veteran teacher who could use his big voice to instantly stop a fight or wrap a crying child in his burly arms. During my elementary school years, a lot of kids didn't have a dad at home, and Mr. Cook was what every kid aspired to.

> During my elementary school years, a lot of kids didn't have a dad at home, and Mr. Cook was what every kid aspired to.

When my mom struggled to make ends meet or had trouble with my older sister acting out, Mr. Cook lent a listening ear and made sure we had school supplies. When I knew I smelled a gas leak by the oldest part of the school, he believed me and had it checked out. (There was a gas leak, and because he was the one adult to believe me, it was found!)

Even though I knew Mr. Cook and was excited to be in his class, I'd still never had the experience of being a student in his classroom. So when the time came for the awful ritual of reading aloud, followed by requisite mockery from my peers, I expected him to ignore it, like so many teachers had before.

I was wrong.

Instead, Mr. Cook gently stopped me to deliver a message to the class. In the most solemn voice I'd ever heard him use, he said, "Listen to me. We do not make fun of anyone practicing reading out loud. We are all here to learn." Then he looked right at me and said, "You read well. Slow down and don't ever be embarrassed to make a mistake."

After that, the teasing stopped. In Mr. Cook's shielding presence, I was finally able to feel calm in my pursuit of knowledge, an equanimity I hadn't known before. I began practicing reading aloud to my little sister every night. Eventually, I overcame my dyslexia when I read aloud because Mr. Cook gave me a safe space to do that.

Thanks to this huge bear of a man, my confidence finally came out of hibernation. His is the voice in my head that reminds me I don't ever need to be embarrassed for making mistakes while I'm learning a new skill. ▪

SPOTLIGHT

As a tomboy who lived and loved football, I asked to join the boys' team. Ken Walker, my history teacher, who was also the team's coach, replied, "You bet!" I wasn't the greatest, but he certainly made me feel that I was. I even got a letter for my jacket! It was 1973, and Mr. Walker was way before his time. —*Cindy J.*

Teacher
of the Year

ERIN B.

There's a teacher who means the world to me, and she's been my inspiration since I was nothing more than a tiny baby. She's my sister.

We're separated by a whole decade, which has led to a monkey-see, monkey-do kind of relationship. Whatever hobbies she took up, I did my darndest to learn. Whatever she ate, or didn't eat, I did the same. I even copied her questionable 2000s fashion choices. I admired her before I even knew what that word meant.

Throughout my existence—and even more so after our mother passed away—she has shown me where love, kindness, and respect will take you in life.

These days, the only difference is it's not just me under her wings. She has guided thousands of children over the years with love, compassion, and knowledge, and was named teacher of the year multiple times for being so dang good at it. After nearly 10 years of teaching, she began opening up to her students in ways most teachers had already been doing their whole careers. But I guess not so much in Texas.

During a "Get to Know Me" slideshow the first week of school, she shared pictures of her family (me included), her hobbies, and places she'd been. A normal thing to do, right? But because of this, she was plucked from her classroom without warning, hesitation, or any explanation, and placed on administrative leave for more than a year.

Ultimately it was because my sister's family is different. Because she loves a woman and not a man—and she did not hide it, just as a heteronormative teacher would not. When she was asked to resign from her job because of this, she knew she was not the first person to face this decision. And she would not be the last if she did not take a stand.

At a tremendous cost to her own well-being, she forged a path for younger generations and spoke up about what she knew was wrong. What turned into a federal lawsuit became one of her biggest lessons as a teacher. She stood up for what was right, that you shouldn't be afraid to love who you love, and you shouldn't have to hide that.

And she won in the courtroom. A federal judge ruled that her suspension was unconstitutional. Most important, the school district planned a vote to ban discrimination based on sexual orientation.

Just as she taught and continues to teach in her classroom, she made it known that love, kindness, and respect for all humans are values that shall not be compromised—especially when you are facing adversity, being bullied, or looking directly into the eyes of traditional ignorance.

This tiny baby sister could not have asked for a stronger, more inspirational role model. ▪

A Different Drum

FELICIA K.

I f you grow up a tomboy in a conservative community, chances are you'll stick out. Sugar and spice and everything nice? Pass. My parents, progressive in their own right, not only allowed me the space to "be myself"—but also the opportunity to figure out who, exactly, that was.

That said, as soon as I exited their bubble, the pressure to fit in returned. Our town was so traditional in terms of gender roles, and school was like the town in microcosm, distilled to its homogeneous, conformity-driven essence. It's not easy being the square peg in a sea of round holes, so eventually I succumbed to pressure, sanded down my edges, and did my best to fit in.

Then, in ninth-grade English, Mrs. Lanza entered my life. Mrs. Lanza was a feminist with a capital *F*—and though this was a term I was familiar with, I shied away from owning it for myself. Certainly, none of my friends used that language, and I already felt so different that I didn't dare exile myself further by using it myself. The mantra at school was "boys will be boys," and it was used to dismiss problematic behavior. It was easier, safer, to be passive. Because, you know. That's what girls do.

But Mrs. Lanza was unapologetic in her beliefs. Equality, decency, respect—these were the beats of her drum. Though tiny in stature, she had the boldest personality, simultaneously intense and understanding. She was intimidating, sure, but safe—always available to answer questions and help us learn. She commanded that classroom like the captain of a ship, holding everyone accountable to a higher level of work and behavior.

Mrs. Lanza made it very clear gender roles could, and should, be challenged. Ninth grade is a heady time of transition and growth, and kids, still feeling their way in the world, say and do a lot of crazy things. But when that "crazy" took the form of misogyny, racism, or bigotry, Mrs. Lanza did not play. She challenged it head-on, directly and boldly. Seeing her stand up to that sort of talk and behavior—well, that taught us how to do the same.

I was thrilled to see it, because deep down, I'd always known this kind of talk was wrong. Mrs. Lanza showed us what it looked like to protest the status quo, so that when the time came for us to do the same, we could.

It wasn't just talk for her, either. It was a way of life. I vividly remember the moment when she overheard a boy verbally abusing his girlfriend in the hallway. Without missing a beat, she exited the classroom and shut it down. She knew how to get to the root of a problem.

Mrs. Lanza was unapologetic in her beliefs. Equality, decency, respect— these were the beats of her drum.

I maintained my wallflower status for a while longer, but Mrs. Lanza's lessons stayed with me forever. Her voice is loudest in my head when I challenge the norm. As a high school teacher myself now, I understand the job requires you to wear many hats. It's not just about academics; you are also teaching young people how to be in the world. You're teaching them how to recognize, forge, and navigate healthy relationships; how to tackle mental health, world issues, politics, home life—everything. And when my students express their love for me and my class, how safe they feel, I know I've succeeded.

Thank you, Mrs. Lanza, for showing me the way. ∎

Hallelujah

MICHELLE W.

Grade 13 English, Toronto, Canada, 1989. A blistering hot summer day. I am deep in my Goth phase—velvet skirt, Doc Martens, green army jacket. In other words: not dressed for the weather.

But it's not just me. The whole class is dying, wilting like balloons the day after a party, perspiring like old men in a Russian bathhouse. How we'll survive a whole English class in this hothouse of despair: unclear.

Mr. Antonovich, our English teacher, walks in. He's wearing his characteristic uniform of Earth shoes, khaki pants, wrinkled blue shirt: fitting regalia for our newly anointed King of Hades. He's carrying a record player he signed out from the library and sets it up on his desk. The room is thick with humidity.

> I'll never forget that day—the day I was introduced to Leonard Cohen. But more than that, I'll never forget Mr. Antonovich, a teacher who believed education was about more than adhering to a strict lesson plan.

I knew Mr. Antonovich was different my very first day, because when he took attendance, he pronounced my last name—Wasyluk—perfectly. My last name had gone mispronounced my whole life, and rather than consign myself to a lifetime of miserably correcting people, I chose to just go along with it—to pretend it was correct. I must have buried a small part of myself, however, because when Mr. Antonovich pronounced it correctly, I literally jumped out of my chair, as if to say, "Yeah, that's me."

Back in Hades, a drop of makeup-swirled sweat plops on my desk. Mr. Antonovich turns off the lights, drops the blinds, and opens a huge window to encourage a breeze.

"Everyone, clear your desks!"

Moans from around the room. A pop quiz? Was he serious? Our teacher smiles. "Rest your heads on your desks and close your eyes." We do. Then we hear the crackle of a needle on vinyl, and the room fills with the most intriguing voice I'd ever heard—a poetic baritone that growls and purrs, speaking of love and mystery.

I briefly open my eyes to see Mr. Antonovich leaning back in his chair: Earth shoes crossed on his desk, hands behind his head, eyes closed, huge smile on his face.

We stay that way the entire period.

I'll never forget that day—the day I was introduced to Leonard Cohen. But more than that, I'll never forget Mr. Antonovich, a teacher who believed education was about more than adhering to a strict lesson plan. Instead, it could be spontaneous and fluid—like music—like the mind itself. Mr. Antonovich didn't pose as a man with the answers, doling them out to his students like our daily gruel. The way he taught showed us that knowledge was something to discover. Something to unearth through conversation and inquiry.

If it's the human condition to feel misunderstood, then perhaps that feeling is the most profound when we are young. The tragedy is that misunderstood young people often internalize the misunderstanding—they let other people decide who they are. Over time, as we grow up, we grow estranged from our true selves, becoming the living embodiment of a name mispronounced: almost ourselves, but not quite, for the rest of our lives.

Mr. Antonovich didn't let that happen. Instead of "molding" us, the way teachers or parents are wont to do, he let us figure it out. We didn't have to be loud to be heard. We didn't have to be smart. All we had to do was *be*—to sit up in our chairs and declare: Yeah. This is me. ∎

SPOTLIGHT

Miss Martin was a wonder. She figured out each kid's talent, then worked it into her teaching plan. For example, Benny loved marbles so we learned about marbles, glassblowing, leather craft for the bags ... She did this for all of us. Every student was a star! —*Aster M.*

CHAPTER THREE

It's the Little Things

Something small can mean so much

The Best Guy I Know

TOMMY M.

My uncle George lives in a home with a few other people like him. He enjoys a simple life—no smartphones, no internet—so, communication is limited to in-person and old-school landline phone calls. He has a girlfriend—Carol—who he marries about once every two weeks. He tells me she thinks I'm handsome, and I tell him to tell her "thank you." It's not clear whether Carol exists.

My uncle and I have always shared a special bond—my middle name, George, is a point of pride—still, when I was around five years old, I asked my parents what was wrong with him. (I was five, OK? Delicacy wasn't my strong suit.) Anyway, they said nothing was "wrong" with him exactly, but that Uncle George was mentally disabled.

Back in the day, George would periodically ask for my cell phone number and write it down. He'd call a bunch of times and then abruptly stop—because he lost the piece of paper with my number on it. This went on for years, until—at some point, around six years ago—he committed my number to memory. Ever since then, about once an hour from 7 a.m. to 7 p.m., he calls me 10 times a day—without fail—365 days a year. Though I love him quite a bit, I answer maybe two of those phone calls a day.

Our phone calls always follow the same structure, using one of three fantasy realities, courtesy of George's imagination. In one, he's my dad and I'm his son (in this role, he enjoys scolding me for cursing). In another, he's Major Charles Winchester, from the 1970s TV show *M*A*S*H**, and I'm Captain B. J. Hunnicutt, reporting for duty. In the last, we're both lifeguards, strategizing the rescue of a drowning person.

When the phone rings, I always say, "Hello?" as if I don't know who is calling. "Hi, George," I'll say. "It's your dad, George!" Or, "It's Major Winchester!" Or, "This is Tower 1. Tower 2, can you read me?" We go back and forth in character for about a minute and a half—only breaking the bit to laugh hysterically. Then, he'll go quiet.

"You know something, Tommy," he'll say. "I'm just calling to say you're the best guy I know."

"So are you," I reply. "The two of us!"

"The two musketeers! All for one and one for all!"

We both laugh. Then, he'll ask what I'm eating for dinner, or if I'm watching the Mets game, and wraps up telling me he'll call me back at a specific time (he always calls back earlier than he says he will).

This conversation has been repeated verbatim multiple times a day for years now. No matter what's going on in the world—no matter how shaky life's underpinnings—the consistency of these calls is something I can count on. At my most stressed and vulnerable, angry and sad—during painful breakups and professional setbacks—that phone call nevertheless rolls in, allowing me to escape reality for a bit, and just laugh and act like a kid again.

> No matter what's going on in the world—no matter how shaky life's underpinnings—the consistency of these calls is something I can count on.

Because George doesn't understand things at an adult level—he has no idea what I do for work, for example—it's impossible for him to comprehend certain aspects of my life, or to truly attune to whether I'm having a good or bad day. Instead, he's able to bring me the same energy—the same love and acceptance—no matter what. It's an incredible gift. Because I know that even at my worst, when I feel like I'm drowning, I can count on Uncle George—up there in Tower 1—to call down from his perch through his mighty megaphone and tell me I'm the best guy he knows.

It's an act of love that saves me—just a little bit—every single day. ∎

Music to My Ears

RUFFIN J.

When I was growing up in the projects of Orlando, Florida, I went to bed hungry many nights simply because we didn't have enough money to buy more food for our family. It was what it was; I got used to it after a while. Poverty was all I knew.

By the time I reached sixth grade, I'd acquired a nickname due to my crooked and overcrowded teeth: "Shark Bite." My mother couldn't afford braces, and truth be told, I did look a lot like a great white. I tried my best to lean into my misfortune and laugh along with my peers, because honestly, I loved to entertain people (and my teeth really were effed up). Smiling helped me forget the harsh reality of being poor—my clothes were always too small, and my shoes were sometimes held together with masking tape.

In addition to laughter, music also kept me going throughout my childhood and adolescence. So in middle school, I decided to join the school band. On the first day of class, my band teacher said we could either choose an instrument we would like to learn, or he could choose for us. I opted to let him assign me an instrument, mostly because I had no idea what I was doing. He studied me for what felt like an eternity before finally saying, "I believe you would be great on trumpet." Young and naive, I assumed that the instruments would be provided to us.

Nope.

Our school was located in an underserved community that had little to no funding for the arts; even though we had a band, the members had to rent their instruments on a monthly basis. My heart sank. I knew there was no way my mother could afford another bill on her plate, when we were already struggling to make ends meet. It took a lot of effort for me to smile through the remainder of that day. It felt like the odds were always stacked against me.

When I got home, I sheepishly told my mom about how I'd joined the school band and that I needed to rent a trumpet. I tried to keep the excitement out of my voice, but she must have picked up on it. Hell, maybe she said yes because I'd always been a good kid who stayed out of trouble and did what I was told. Either way, I was shocked when she agreed to take me to a local music store. I was so happy I felt like my chest could burst.

Throughout sixth grade, I had to return my instrument three times because my mother couldn't afford to keep up the monthly payments. Somehow, she always found a way to get it back so I could keep playing. Music was one of the only things that made me happy; when I was performing, the whole world went quiet, and it was just my trumpet and me.

When I was in seventh grade, we stopped having to return the trumpet to the music store; I assumed it was because my mother was finally able to afford the payment plan. I played the shit out of that instrument until I graduated from high school.

The summer after my freshman year of college, my mother asked me to clean out the hallway closet for her. As I rummaged through boxes of papers, I stumbled upon a letter from Allegro Music Centre, dated 2009—the year I was in seventh grade. Tears welled in my eyes as I read it:

Dear Mrs. Ruffin:

I have decided to forgive the rent on Jacques's trumpet. You do not have to pay me anymore for the trumpet. It is yours to play.

However, if Jacques drops out of band and stops playing the trumpet, will you return it to me so I can give it to some other deserving student?

I have been through bad times like you. But remember, tough times never last. Tough people do.

Sincerely,
James W. Jones

The only reason I was able to continue pursuing my love of music is because of the shop owner's generosity (and my mother's persistence). He could have repossessed or even reported the failure to make timely payments. Instead, he decided to encourage my mother—and me. What a beautiful lesson.

Tough times never last, but tough people do. ∎

SPOTLIGHT

I was pumping gas one winter, and an older gentleman at the next pump used the windshield squeegee to wash off my salt-crusted taillights. I'd like to think it's something my dad would have done if he'd lived long enough to see me drive. —*Kristen B.*

Adjusting Together

AZIZA M.

Moving from a big house with a sprawling yard into a tiny two-bedroom apartment is a major adjustment for anyone—but with kids, it's damn near impossible.

My sons and I were living with my mom outside the city limits when I started dating a man who turned out to be an absolute nutjob. Ryder, my older son, was five at the time; my younger son, Lennox, was three. I didn't have time to prepare them, or even to pack all our things. We just fled, moving quickly into an apartment in an undisclosed location where I knew we'd be safe.

The boys didn't understand why we had to leave our home with their grandmother, and it was tough for me to explain in an age-appropriate way. I was terrified all the time, juggling work and motherhood, collecting evidence for the police, wondering if and when my stalker would be arrested. Ryder sensed the stress and sweetly encouraged me with pep talks, while Lennox, quieter by nature, offered lots of snuggles and hugs.

> One day, the boys were playing and hit their bedroom wall with such force that it caused something in our neighbor's bedroom to fall down. Angrily, she stomped over and knocked on the door.

The concept of apartment living wasn't something my rambunctious, country-raised sons understood; they just couldn't wrap their minds around the fact that other people lived directly next to and above us. Their bedroom shared a wall with our neighbor's bedroom, and every time I heard them jumping on the bed or running around in there, I cringed.

Our neighbor lived alone with several cats, and she wasn't accustomed to loud children. Every time we greeted her in passing, she seemed stern and aloof, rarely smiling. One day, the boys were playing and hit their bedroom wall with such force that it caused something in our neighbor's bedroom to fall down. Angrily, she stomped over and knocked on the door.

When I saw her, my heart sank. I knew she was mad, and I didn't blame her one bit—I'd be upset too! I apologized profusely, explaining that the kids weren't used to apartment life yet, and gave her a brief rundown of why we were there in the first place. She seemed to soften a bit once I explained, and I assured her I would do a better job of keeping the volume level down.

After she left, I sat the boys down and managed to explain how apartments work in a way they could understand, and why the neighbor could hear everything they were doing. Once they realized she literally shared a bedroom wall with them, they felt terrible, and asked if we could give her flowers as an apology. I told them that was a great idea, and took the opportunity to write her a card, apologizing again and assuring her I'd work hard to help them adjust.

My kids and I left to run some errands, and when we returned, we found that our neighbor had left some alphabet cookies with a sweet card:

> *Thank you so much for the flowers and card. It was very thoughtful. I appreciate it and we will adjust together. :)*

Well, I thought that was beautiful as hell. It was a good reminder that you never know what people are going through. Most adults, at one time or another, have either been in my shoes or my neighbor's. Both are hard. (And, at times, too loud.)

It's been two years since then, and we are doing great. Domestic violence ruins lives, but I refused to let it ruin ours. I'm raising two kind, compassionate boys who will one day make the world a better, safer place. ∎

Brocc On

KRISTINA R.

I'm walking my bike home like a pack mule, with a four-year-old strapped into the back seat and a two-year-old slung on my back. It's the season of plums and apples here in Denmark, but I don't have time to relax with a cider or a nice glass of dark wine. It's straight home for dinner, maybe a little break before bedtime. After a full day studying at the university, I'm already looking forward to lights out.

I come to the largest intersection in town: two busy lanes going opposite directions, each roaring with traffic. I'm in the home stretch, crossing with the rest of the crowd, when my four-year-old screams. I whip around with my heart in my throat, absorbing the sight of my small son's wailing face. But he's all right. Right? He's fine.

But then I look down. A big fat broccoli plushie grins up at me from the asphalt. It's my son's favorite toy. He's shrieking like he's lost an arm, practically clawing out of his seat to get at it. But I'm stuck in the middle of an intersection, hands glued to the bike that—if I let go—would topple over, screaming son included. Traffic begins to move, and the broccoli's grin morphs into something desperate: *Save me.* But I can't! My son wails like a siren.

Then, the largest biker I'd ever seen in my life slows to a halt. Despite a green light, all lanes remain frozen while the biker marches toward me, brow furrowed, jaw set. Clad in head-to-toe leather, he has a mass of disheveled, shoulder-length hair and a beard that could rival Hagrid's. So daunting is his approaching bulk that even my son snaps to attention—he practically squeaks in his seat.

My heart pounds. Leather-clad bikers with Viking beards would seem to rank relatively low on the tolerance meter—and seeing as I pretty much qualify as a human roadblock, I imagine his patience has been tested. His eyes burn at me in their sockets as he dips to the ground, scooping up Broccoli with surprising tenderness. He hands it to my sniffling son and smiles.

Relief washes over me. Dealing with crying children is normal for me, but getting help isn't. I tell my son to say thank you, but he's too terrified. It'll take two whole minutes before he works up the nerve to speak, and by that time the biker's long gone.

My son still recalls that moment in awe, bringing it up again and again out of the blue—utterly amazed: "That motorcycle man picked up my Broccoli!" As the cliché goes: Not all heroes wear capes. Sometimes they wear leather. ∎

The Art of Connection

MELANIE K.

The first year we introduced the intergenerational Opening Minds Through Art (OMA) program to our high school art students, they were a little hesitant about the idea. The program paired them with residents in long-term care homes who are living with dementia; together, the two generations would create abstract artworks. Most of our students had zero experience or exposure to seniors living with this difficult disease and weren't sure what to expect. But because of the program's name, it was no surprise that they quickly felt the rewards of this unique connection.

The students met with their senior partners and created beautiful art each week. Working hand over hand, they gently guided them through the artistic process: Would you like red or blue? Do you want to use a brush or a sponge?

Providing choice to people with dementia—even something as simple as which tool to engage—offers a sense of agency: fundamental to human dignity. The abstract art pieces became a form of communication, a chance for their families to glean a sense of their inner lives, pure and undistorted. Every choice and expression was a reminder: I'm still here.

The program took off and flourished, attracting more student volunteers than we could accommodate. My students looked forward to their weekly visits, having connected quickly with their new senior partners. The love and energy in that collaborative art space were palpable.

Until COVID hit.

Entry into care homes ceased, schools closed, and the program was shuttered. The high school students were stuck at home, away from their peers and their classroom routines, navigating this new, unknown world as best they could. They processed their experiences and isolation through artwork, even if emailing me their pieces was the only means of display. It was wonderful to see their creativity even though we had to be apart.

At the same time, we were hearing how devastated the long-term care home experience was for our senior art partners. Weighed down with the thought of such heartbreak and isolation, I realized that there was only one solution: to keep the partnership going. I asked my students to create art that the residents might enjoy, then printed their artwork as mini posters and delivered them to 10 long-term care homes in our city. At a time when visitors were forbidden and all connection to the outside world was lost, we found a way to say, "We're thinking of you. We want to add some sunshine into your day and stay connected."

The artwork was warmly welcomed. One center's recreational therapist asked the residents their views of the artwork and compiled poems from their answers. She then had her residents make abstract paintings to send back to our students. What had started as a simple delivery became a collaborative back-and-forth. I had prints made of the seniors' paintings, then asked my students to design illustrations on top of the seniors' art. One drew coral and jellyfish over a resident's abstract watercolor. Another inked drawings of a flowery meadow over splashes from the resident's paintbrush.

Creativity from both sets of artists combined into an expression of friendship through art. What had started as a simple delivery became a meaningful conversation. It was a reconnection. Together, they found a new language—a language louder than COVID, more powerful than words—that transformed art into communication and elevated communication into art. ∎

SPOTLIGHT

I was in my first year of law school and driving home late at night, stressed after studying all day for finals. I was stopped at a traffic light, crying a bit, when a guy knocked on my passenger side window, holding out a bouquet of flowers. He was driving a florist delivery truck, noticed I was upset, and said he hoped the flowers would make me feel better. That was more than 30 years ago, and about once a week I think of him and wish him well.
—*Emily W.*

The Promise of Pancakes

CURTIS K.

It was peak pandemic in San Francisco, and I was feeling lonely. Truth be told, I'd been feeling that way for a while, but quarantining certainly didn't help the issue. As far as I could tell, it wasn't just me; I wasn't alone in my aloneness. The entire city had a bleak vibe—and for once, you couldn't blame the fog.

I decided to do something about it.

From 2009 to 2015, I ran a successful crème brûlée business. Man, people really lined up for that burnt custard goodness. So I figured, why not try my hand at something similar, but different? Something equally warm and delicious, but less French, more comforting, like—Ooh!—pancakes. Everyone likes pancakes, I thought, or at least the idea of pancakes. To test my theory, I decided to throw a citywide pancake party and see who showed up.

> Everyone likes pancakes, I thought, or at least the idea of pancakes. To test my theory, I decided to throw a citywide pancake party and see who showed up.

Not being much of an email guy, I decided to go old-school—papering the city with posters including my address, the date, and the time. I told people to prepare for not only the best pancakes, but also the richest chocolate chips, the sweetest maple syrup, and the creamiest butter this side of the Rio Grande. I also added a short disclaimer that my wife said I was getting weird and needed to make new friends.

Did part of me worry people would think I had batter for brains? Sure! But then I thought, Sometimes, you gotta do things out of the ordinary to achieve the extraordinary—to knock folks out of autopilot and into living life.

Anyway, those posters seemed to do the trick, because by the time I flipped my first flapjack, people were lining up, excited to check out Pancakepalooza. Enthusiasm only grew from there, from a modest short stack to a veritable tower. In the end, I made pancakes for more than 75 people—kids with their moms and dads, elderly couples, hungry teens, and every type of person in between. I'm telling you, it was pure joy: after all that isolation, a sense of community at last. And all because some guy put up posters promising pancakes.

It might sound corny, but it felt like the best part of being an American: to gather and bond with a bunch of strangers and to celebrate what we have in common—pancakes!—rather than choke down the tasteless, dry cereal of sticking with what we know.

I've now hosted several pancake parties—even kept them going while traveling cross-country—and you can bet I've got more ideas cooking. Because, though I may love making food, it's the people that make it magic. At the end of the day (or in the beginning, if it's breakfast), we're all hungry to connect. ■

A Gift From the Heart

CHANTEL C.

When I was 21, I went on a trip to Dubai with my best friends. We traveled all over the city: the Burj Khalifa, the desert, spas, clubs.

On my very last day, en route to the airport, I lost my ID. I was upset it happened on the last day of the trip (which in retrospect seems lucky, given how much we'd moved around). But I remained calm because I still had my passport. Eventually, I made it back to Woodland Hills, California, where I lived, and applied for a new license.

One day months later, I entered the lobby of my building to pick up my mail. As I sorted through bills and flyers, I landed on an envelope that looked like it'd been through hell: yellowed, dusty, and bent, with no return address. I remember sliding open the top with my fingernail when something slipped out, falling at my feet. I looked down. It was the ID I'd lost in Dubai.

I gasped and scanned the envelope for a note. There one was, written in beautiful script:

> *I pray this reaches you. I found your license on the seat of a cab in Dubai. The driver gave me his blessing to return it to you. God bless you in your travels always.*
> *—Mike*

I was dumbfounded. I never thought I'd see that ID again and couldn't believe it had successfully traveled such a great distance. But more than that, I was struck by the kindhearted man who sent it to me—someone I had no opportunity to thank, because there was no return address.

Whoever Mike was, one thing was certain: He had no expectation of receiving something in return. He took the time to mail an expendable piece of plastic as if it weren't expendable at all, but rather an object of deep meaning and value to another person—an action that had deep meaning to me.

In my life, I know, I'll replace old licenses with new ones. But this one—and what it symbolizes—is irreplaceable. ■

Good Hair Day

SHARON B.

It's a bright day in St. Louis, Missouri, a few days before my older son's wedding. Soon, we'll be sitting at banquet tables festooned with bouquets, blitzed by champagne and twinkle lights, tearing up the dance floor in our flouncy dresses and tailored suits, bow ties and blowouts.

Right now, however, we're at a taco joint, just hanging out, brushing chip dust off our laps, yukking it up over carnitas and guac. It's 90 degrees Fahrenheit—Coca-Cola weather—so, I get up from the table and beeline for the vending machine. As I pause to fish coins out of my purse, a lady sitting with her friend at a nearby table calls out—"Girl! I love your haircut. It's so cute!"

I laugh ruefully. "It is!" The friend insists. She tells me I'm "brave."

At this point, my hair's maybe half an inch long, close-cropped, like Mia Farrow in *Rosemary's Baby*. Unlike Mia's, my haircut wasn't part of a larger story in which I'm manipulated into the arms of the devil. Not literally, anyway. But I'd definitely endured a certain kind of hell.

Still, these ladies don't know that. They think I'm edgy, cool, brave, and I feel compelled to set them straight. "Thank you," I say. "But I can't take credit for this haircut. It was just kind of handed to me on a [expletive] platter."

I was diagnosed just under a year ago, at 53. No kids in the house—they'd all fled the nest at that point. It was just me, my husband, and our new, possibly homicidal roommate, triple-negative breast cancer. This new roommate didn't pay rent; instead, it took a toll. Security, self-esteem, sanity, strength: Every day, every hour, cancer came to collect.

In light of this life-altering news, you might have expected my first question to have been something more profound than "Am I going to lose my hair?" I've since learned it's pretty common—I mean, as a first question—especially among women. Because it's not just hair, right? It's part of who we are.

When I was a kid, my hair was my crowning glory. This was back in the 1970s, so picture Jan Brady: parted down the middle, stick-straight, super blond—so long that at one point I could sit on it. I was the youngest, so my mom babied me a bit, brushing it, braiding it, matching my ponytail holders to my outfits. I was so proud. In a way, losing my hair meant losing that girl—a beloved part of myself to which I'd been tethered by literal strands, each one now about to fall out.

Two weeks into chemo, my hair was everywhere—my shoulders, my pillowcase, the couch, the floor. Little traitors, abandoning ship just when the sailing got rough. I was determined to regain some sense of control, take matters into my own hands (plus, all that hair was gross), so I called up my daughter-in-law. At the time, she and my son lived close by. He was in the Navy, and my daughter-in-law is in charge of keeping his hair cut short. I didn't want a stranger to be the one to cut my hair, so I asked her if she'd be willing to do the honors—to come aboard as barber in chief.

"Lexi," I said over the phone. "Today's the day."

Hours later, we were in my kitchen: the onetime locus point of a thousand chaotic mornings, countless hurried breakfasts, sandwiches rolled into tinfoil, high chairs taken in and out of storage. I sat in a chair. Lexi put a sheet on the floor. She shaved my head right there, starting at the front and buzzing a path over the top of my head. Blond hair drifted to the floor. A moment of silence.

> Lexi put a sheet on the floor. She shaved my head right there, starting at the front and buzzing a path over the top of my head. Blond hair drifted to the floor. A moment of silence.

"You look just like Ben Franklin," my husband said at last. And just like that, we were all laughing.

Lexi wadded up the sheet and kicked it out the back door. I just sort of sat there, feeling my head—delaying the inevitable. Finally, I got up, went to the living room, and looked in the mirror. They let me have my space. I cried. Then, we had dinner.

A few weeks after chemo ends, once your body clears it out of its system, you start getting this peach fuzz. By the time my son's wedding rolled around, my peach fuzz had graduated into something resembling a buzz cut. Thank goodness, the cancer was kicked, but so was my hair. To me, it felt like a flashing neon arrow: CANCER. So, for the day of the wedding, I resolved to wear a wig. True, it would be itchy and uncomfortable, but the last thing I wanted to do was draw attention to myself and potentially bum people out. This day was about the bride and groom, not the gloom and doom.

Anyway, I end up explaining all this to the ladies at the taco joint. The whole damn saga just came pouring out. I'm crying. They're crying. I mean, sometimes, when I picture it, I can't help but laugh. (Three random ladies bawling like idiots while salsa music plays in the background? Admit it, it's funny.)

But here's the thing: Those women stood their ground. Absolutely refused to budge on the main point. My haircut is so cute. Truly! They loved it.

A couple years after the wedding, that restaurant closed down for the pandemic. When they reopened, I experienced this surge of joy, like, Oh good, I'll see those women again!

But I'm not going to see those women again. And even if I did, I wouldn't recognize them. They wouldn't recognize me. It was just, you know, this moment in time. That impacted us. Impacted me.

It's a moment I remember fondly every time I look through my son's wedding photos. There I am, "cute" haircut included. Which is to say, I didn't end up wearing a wig that day. Thanks to those ladies, I had the confidence to go without it. ■

SPOTLIGHT

She paid for my car to get out of the impound lot. I was her co-worker for all of two weeks. We've been best friends ever since. Going on 15 years.
—*Jessica M.*

A Brighter Shade of Pink

ELLE H.

When I was a little girl growing up in a suburb just south of Nashville, I grew accustomed to seeing some interesting things.

It wasn't unusual to run into country music stars in church or at the hardware store, decked out in big hats and cowboy boots. They received the same treatment as everybody else in town, which is probably why they liked living there. Several members of the Grand Ole Opry lived in our neighborhood; one of them even had a pet leopard (or maybe it was a jaguar) that got loose on multiple occasions, running wild through manicured lawns.

Tennessee is a wonderful place to live. Southern hospitality is real, and it was a tradition my mother was proud to uphold. She was a beautiful woman, stylish and elegant, and I loved accompanying her on errands. I was a shy child and would quietly follow behind her, mimicking her every move. She trained us from an early age to look people in the eye and extend a polite greeting with a smile, no matter what.

So you can imagine my delight when one day, while shopping at the SupeRx drugstore, I made eye contact with what appeared to be a real-life princess in the makeup aisle.

The woman was just as beautiful as my mother, wearing denim and rhinestones from head to toe, with gorgeous blond hair and

> You can imagine my delight when one day, while shopping at the SupeRx drugstore, I made eye contact with what appeared to be a real-life princess in the makeup aisle.

long, red nails. Her teeth were perfectly white and straight, and she had dimples. I was mesmerized.

Normally, adults don't pay any mind to small children, but this lady quickly noticed me noticing her and asked my mother if it would be OK if I could help her decide on a shade of lipstick. I couldn't believe it—she wanted *my* opinion? This seemed like a very big, very serious responsibility. I felt so special!

My chest swelled with pride as I studied the tubes in her hand, considering which one I liked best, finally settling on the brighter, more obnoxious shade of pink. She conspiratorially asked my mother if it was all right for her to get one for me, too.

Dolly Parton bought two tubes of lipstick that day—one for me and one for her. As she waved goodbye, she asked me to think of her every time I put on my lipstick, and she would do the same. Because of that encounter, I've spent my whole life looking for ways to make a child feel special.

And I also know the value of an outstanding lip color. ■

The Camaro

ERIN M.

E very so often in life, a good person comes along—someone
you don't know, but does good by you anyway. That happened
to me when Cory, the current owner of my dad's old Camaro, came
to visit.

We'd only met once, in 2019, when we sold him the car, signing
paperwork and handing over the keys. The Camaro was a 1967
classic, painted a beautiful shade of plum that shifted color depend-
ing on the light. Clutching the keys, Cory said he couldn't wait to
have a car that he and his small son could "grow into together." I
smiled, knowing what he meant.

When I was a kid, I'd be out the door the minute my dad started
the engine, ready to slide into the smooth, upholstered front seat
for our next weekend adventure. Where we were headed—the market, a nearby park, around the block—was anyone's guess. In a car
like that, with your favorite person at the wheel, destinations don't
matter; it's all about the ride. Windows down, we'd cruise along
to the mixtape he'd so patiently made, selecting his favorite classic
songs from his record albums. I still remember the first track—
"Free Ride"—by the Edgar Winter Group.

When we sold the car, we left that tape inside the cassette player.

It warms my heart to imagine it there—like my dad's spirit is still in the car.

In the spring of 2007, my father was diagnosed with liver cancer; the prognosis was three months. By the end of summer, he was still powering through, living on borrowed time. I quit my job to become his caregiver and was home with him around the clock.

One day, around the time summer imperceptibly shifts into fall, my dad came up to me and said, "Come on—I'm going to teach you how to drive the Camaro." My body flooded with emotion—with excitement, nerves, and, most prominently, a kind of heart-sinking dread. We didn't say it out loud—it was an unspoken understanding. He was going to die. But not without teaching me how to drive his car first.

I drove stick for the first time that afternoon, cruising around town for hours, sometimes peeling out as I learned to let out the clutch—Dad in the front seat, where I used to sit as a kid. It was the first and last time I drove the Camaro with him as a passenger. He was gone about a month later.

> In a car like that, with your favorite person at the wheel, destinations don't matter; it's all about the ride.

Fifteen years passed; the car was also long gone. It was Father's Day, and I was sitting on my couch, in my own house, with my dog, Willow. I'd just moved back to my childhood neighborhood, right up the street from my mom, and was enjoying some solitude on what can sometimes feel like a somber day. As I sat, soaking in the quiet, I heard a classic car come up the road. I craned my neck to see out the window. My jaw dropped. With a surge of adrenaline, I immediately called my mom and told her the Camaro had just driven past my house. Confused, she went to look out her window and said, "It's here—it's in front of my house!"

I grabbed my car keys and ran out barefoot.

Cory had already rung my mother's doorbell by the time he saw me barrel up the driveway. I could barely put my car in park, didn't bother shutting the door. I just walked right up to him and, without hesitation, gave this virtual stranger a tear-filled hug. He gave me a squeeze back, and that's when I knew he'd made this visit—on Father's Day—for me.

Cory had poured a ton of new work into the car but chose to keep a small dimple at the front of the hood, made years ago by a stone kicked up from the road. Like a beauty mark, he observed, it added character. Before he left, my fingers grazed the small dent as if to say hello.

I never hear anyone talk about this, but I'm going to share it, because I feel pretty certain that it's something we, the bereaved, all do. When we see someone who looks like our loved one from afar—someone has the same laugh, or drives the same car—we pretend, for a second or two, that it really is them. That they're here. That they never left.

So that's the gift I received on my 15th Father's Day without my father—to imagine, if only for a few seconds, that as this young father drove away, it was my father behind the wheel—taking the Camaro out for a spin, just like he'd always done. ∎

SPOTLIGHT

He called me every day during my addiction. I was living on the street, and everyone had given up or tried to shame me into sobriety. But my friend, who is now my best friend, called without judgment or preaching, to be silly and let me cry if needed. His calls made my dark days bright. They made me feel important—important enough to get help. I have been clean for five years. *—Amber B.*

Ray of Sunshine

ERIC L.

My freshman year of college didn't go quite as planned. I was reeling from my first big heartbreak, still processing the somewhat recent death of my father, and adjusting to college life. I was living in a new town with all new friends who were more acquaintances than anything else. I didn't like the idea of opening up to people I didn't really know with all these feelings.

One particularly bad day, I cut out of class early to sit outside and get some fresh air. I was deep in thought, head leaned into one hand, staring at the table where I was sitting, when I heard a kind voice say, "You look like you could use a friend." I jerked my head up, and there she was: Holly. Smiling out from under a crop of flaming red hair, she looked like a ray of sunshine in overalls and a bright yellow shirt.

Holly's sincere kindness truly helped brighten my mood. As we talked, she sat with me and I realized just how long it had been since I'd had a conversation with another person who genuinely seemed to care about why I was having a bad day. She was right— I did need a friend, more than I even realized. Just having another person offer me a space where I could share my troubles was an immense gift.

Such a small moment in time. Such a small act of kindness. Twenty years later, we're still going strong. ■

Mothering for Mothers

LISA D.

Why do so many women, particularly mothers, say no when others offer to help? It's like a neon sign lit up by our psyches—DO NOT SAY YES—no matter how exhausted, hungry, or overburdened we feel. It's as if we'd rather let ourselves burn out than remove one watt of power from that Vegas-bright sign in our minds.

I have to imagine this is why the observant woman on our international flight from France to New York didn't ask for permission before jumping in to help me: She just knew. My children were one and two at the time. My husband had stayed behind in Europe, so I was parenting solo, taking the children to visit family for the Fourth of July. I couldn't wait to introduce them to everyone back home.

Assuming we made it through the flight.

While well-rested passengers smiled at my babies and played peekaboo, I willed my eyes to stay open, longing to prop them open with clothespins, like they do in cartoons. I relished being a mother, but I was cooked. And hungry. Kind of an ironic combination when you think about it.

The flight attendant stopped at my seat, dinner in tow, multiple times. Each time I had to ask her to come back later, as I was either feeding one child or the other. I was pretty much at my limit, when a fellow passenger with a Texas drawl came up to my row. "Let me hold your baby," she said. "You have to eat your dinner." I protested—but she held firm.

> Funnily enough, mothering is exactly what many new mothers need most—and this kind woman provided it in spades.

"You need your strength," she said. And that was that.

I will never, ever forget her self-initiative and compassion. She didn't ask permission to help; she just did it. Funnily enough, mothering is exactly what many new mothers need most—and this kind woman provided it in spades.

It's been nearly 20 years since that flight, and yet this experience stays with me. My fellow passenger helped me realize it's OK to ask for help—and accept it when someone offers. ∎

SPOTLIGHT

I was working at a dead-end job when I was 19. When it was my last day, the manager said, "I don't wanna see you back here." He meant that I had way more potential than working at this place, and that was an encouragement I really needed back then. It's been 17 years and I never ended up back there. But I always remember that Dave believed in me when I didn't even believe in myself. *—Kelsey E.*

Serenity Now

LIZE V.

There's something so enchanting about the way I imagine mermaids move through water, their shimmery tails a perfect balance of strength and grace. They're beautiful, strong, and impossible to catch—all appealing qualities. Of course, *actual* marine life mesmerizes me, too: jellyfish, seahorses, starfish. But when it comes to mermaids—well, I'm fully obsessed.

For as long as I can remember, I've loved them; every birthday or special occasion, I was given a mermaid item. My bedroom was decked out with mermaid bedding, my bathroom held mermaid-shaped soaps, and my belongings were covered in mermaid stickers. But one item sticks out: one I've carried with me all the way into adulthood.

I discovered her one day when I was six, while browsing the local flea market with my father. We went there often, and I loved admiring the interesting trinkets, all conveniently displayed at my eye level. I was perusing a tabletop laden with rocks when I looked up and stopped in my tracks. Gripping my father's hand, I pointed and whispered, "Look!"

> I was perusing a tabletop laden with rocks when I looked up and stopped in my tracks. Gripping my father's hand, I pointed and whispered, "Look!"

It was the most beautiful thing I'd seen: a solid white statue of a mermaid with a sweeping tail resting on a rock. I absolutely had to have her.

We didn't have much money, especially to spend on things like mermaid statues. (And even as a six-year-old, I understood mermaid statues were probably nonessential to survival.) My father asked the man at the booth how much she cost, and I could tell by his expression that it was too much.

My father told me the mermaid was really heavy. But, he added, if the statue's still there when we finish looking around, maybe we can bring it home. Looking back, I'm positive he'd hoped I'd forget about it. But, like I said, I was obsessive. And though I clamped my mouth shut and refrained from bugging him about it while we finished browsing, I never stopped thinking about her. She was mine.

When we were finally done and it was time to leave, I reminded him that we needed to go back and see if she was still there. He sighed, and we headed back over to find that someone else was already in the process of buying her. I watched in horror as the interloper picked her up, hoisted her to his chest, and fished some money (no pun intended) from his pants pocket.

I must have made an audible sound of disappointment, because the stranger noticed. I turned to my father sadly. "See?" I said. "I knew if we waited, she'd be gone."

The man asked if I was referring to the mermaid he was holding, and I nodded, staring at my silly human feet. Without hesitation, the man presented me with the statue. I looked up at him—mouth open, eyes wide—perhaps resembling a real-life fish more than I'd like to admit. The man refused to accept payment from my father, saying if I wanted the mermaid that much, I should have it.

Currently, the mermaid resides in my living room—a daily visual reminder of that man's spontaneous generosity. I named her Serenity, and seeing her reminds me to be kind whenever possible—because even a seemingly small gesture, like buying a mermaid for a little girl, can hold enormous meaning. Mermaids may not exist in real life, but good people do. I'll never stop believing in that. ▪

Glory Days

INGER R.

I was 25, working in a small tourist office in Dublin. I loved my job—or, at least, I had loved it until that morning. Now, it seemed more like some kind of cosmic punishment.

Again and again, the entrance door swung open, ushering in yet another group of friends decked out in bright concert tees, faces aglow with Christmas-morning anticipation. It seemed as though all of Ireland was going to this concert—everyone except me, the sad girl with the side braid. Trapped behind purgatory's front desk, I was tasked for all eternity with giving people directions to heaven—a heaven from which I, due to the cardinal sin of being young and broke, was excluded. The name of this heaven, you ask?

Bruce Springsteen.

I'd always liked his music—my dad would play the greatest hits album in our car during road trips. Later, a boyfriend introduced me to his more "obscure" works, songs whose edges, saved from the sanding down of constant radio play, still remained sharp, surprising.

But it wasn't until I saw Springsteen live in concert—in Holland, where I grew up—that I transformed into a true fan. Whereas before his music connected me to my dad, or to my boyfriend, it now connected me to myself. The boyfriend and I eventually parted ways—but not me and Bruce. Ours was a love "faithful and true," as Bruce would sing to me. Well, not only to me, turns out. Apparently, he was having an affair—with all of Ireland.

Of course—being the consummate professional—I swallowed my jealousy and did my job, handing each concertgoer a high-lighted bus map to Croke Park with a bubbly (if slightly manic) "Have fun!" It was the right decision, I reminded myself—not spending what little money I had on an exorbitantly expensive ticket to a concert I'd already seen.

Except I hadn't already seen it! It's like what they say about not being able to put your hand into the same river twice. No concert is ever the same. Because music, like water, is always changing, moving forward—born to run.

The door swung open, yet again, revealing a cheerful-looking woman in her 60s with a cloud of strawberry blond hair. She wasn't wearing a concert tee. As she approached the counter, I pleaded silently. Just, please, be from Canada. Ask me how to get to Blarney Castle. Any place but—

"Hello!" she greeted me in the local brogue. My heart sunk. "Can you please tell me how to get to Croke Park?"

I'm not sure why—maybe because it was the end of the day, or because she had such a sweet, open face—but, of all the people who entered the office that day, she was the only one with whom I had a conversation. I mean, a real one—going deeper than "How can I help you?" and "Have fun!"

We connected over our love of Springsteen, how incredible he is in concert, the unbelievable energy he's able to conjure and sustain. I told her how I'd debated buying a ticket, but resolved not to, finally, choosing "fiscal responsibility" over Fan Brain. I told her I regretted my decision. She nodded, sympathetic, but with averted eyes, reaching into her handbag—which I interpreted as a sign she had to get going. I was about to tell her "Have fun!"—but she slid something across the counter.

I stared at the ticket, stunned.

"Here you go," she said. She just happened to have an extra ticket, she explained—her friend couldn't go last minute—and she'd planned to sell it at the gate. But now, she wanted me to have

> She nodded, sympathetic, but with averted eyes, reaching into her handbag—which I interpreted as a sign she had to get going. I was about to tell her "Have fun!"—but she slid something across the counter.

it. I stammered out something stupid, offering to pay—but she refused. She just wanted me to have it.

I thanked her and thanked her (it's possible, looking back, in addition to expressing gratitude, I was trying to convince myself, through sheer repetition, that this was real). She just smiled, as if to say, Your happiness is all the payment I need.

Yeah. Let's just say—there were two Bosses that day.

As soon as she left, it was go time. My co-workers, none of whom were Springsteen fans, were nevertheless freaking out. It was like Charlie finding the golden ticket, Dorothy pushing open the gray door into a world of Technicolor.

I called up a friend who I knew loved Bruce as much as I did, and who shared my despondency over not being able to go, due to financial constraints. I proposed we go together: buy another ticket at the gate and split the cost. She was ecstatic. It wasn't just the fact that we were going—it was the sheer miraculousness of it all, the sudden turn of events. This was happening.

My boyfriend (a new one) met me at work with an emergency ham and cheese sandwich—one of the many reasons I'd later marry him. I had no time to change, so I wore my work clothes, hoovering the sandwich in the back seat of a taxi while my friend tore through Dublin on her bicycle. Sure enough, when we got to the venue, ticket hawkers were outside, asking loads. But one blessed man sold us a ticket at cost. Barely had money exchanged hands, when "Badlands"—courtesy of a thousand loudspeakers—came booming across the sky.

My friend and I took off running toward the music, the stars of our own music video—a music video called life. We started singing along, laughing, dashing through the halls of Croke Park, stopping once—to ask security how to get to our seats.

The gorgeous irony of the moment did not escape me. Because of one wonderful woman—a stranger whose simple act of generosity opened up my life—I was now asking for directions, not giving them. ∎

Joy Ride

NICOLE C.

I don't consider myself a runner. It's not my favorite thing to do—I actually prefer rock climbing—but sometimes I go for a run when I'm feeling overwhelmed.

One day when I was in the middle of a trail run, I encountered an older couple riding their bikes. As they passed, I noticed they were probably both in their mid-60s, and that a custom adult-size seat was attached to the back of the husband's bike. It looked like what you might install for a toddler to ride on, except it was large enough for a grown man.

Perched on the back of that bike was a man who looked to be in his 80s, white hair blowing in the wind as his son pedaled. The old man's hands gripped the sides of the seat, and he had a wide grin on his face. It looked like he was having the best day of his (very long) life.

My steps slowed, then finally stopped, as I watched them roll by. When they were out of sight, I realized I was smiling myself, simply from witnessing another person's joy. ▪

SPOTLIGHT

I was completing my bachelor of education, and my professor, Mr. Mac-Gregor, said that I was the kind of person he'd like to have teach his kids. I enjoyed a 30-year teaching career. And I still have that 42-year-old note.
—*Debra C.*

The Gift of Encouragement

DANIELLE R.

New motherhood is absolutely terrifying.

People talk about it like it's some kind of enchanting walk through a butterfly garden, but the reality is exhausting, draining, and anxiety-ridden—especially if you have a newborn struggling to adapt to life outside of the womb.

Lucas, our first, arrived via C-section at the end of 2021. It took a while for my stitches to heal, so when I left the house with the baby for the first time on my own, he was several weeks old.

Our maiden voyage was to the pediatrician's office. I felt confident about my knowledge of how the car seat worked—it just clicked in and out of the base attached to the back seat of our SUV. I'd watched my husband take it out and snap it into the stroller multiple times, but I left 20 minutes early for our appointment, just in case. You never know what might happen with a newborn.

I pulled into a parking spot right in front of the doctor's office, turned off the engine, and took a breath. I was exhausted. Lucas had gastroesophageal reflux disease (GERD) and jaundice, and cried all the time. He was underweight, and I never slept. It worried me he was so skinny; I felt like I wasn't doing this mom thing right.

Once I'd gathered my thoughts and felt ready to go, I went around to Lucas's side, opened the car door, and tried to lift the car seat out of the base. It wouldn't budge. I pulled and tugged and pressed the release button, straining my stitches as beads of sweat popped out along my forehead. Lucas began to stir and then started to fuss, probably wondering what the hell his mother was doing. The damn seat would not come out, no matter what I did, and I began to panic.

I looked at the time—we were going to be late for our appointment. I practiced how I would explain our tardiness: I am so sorry, doctor. I couldn't get the baby out of the car. How inept was I?! Adding insult to injury, Lucas was really crying now—like he could tell how bad I was at this entire thing.

Feeling desperate, I looked up and spotted a woman walking through the parking lot with three children in tow. Without even thinking, I yelled to her for help.

She didn't hesitate, hurrying right over, her children scurrying behind. The car seat really was jammed and wouldn't come out, so she suggested putting Lucas in the stroller without his car seat. I had no idea that was even possible with such a tiny baby! She gently showed me how to put him in it so that he wouldn't fall out or roll around while it was moving. Before we parted ways, she assured me it would get easier. I wasn't sure I believed her, but I was so grateful that tears welled in my eyes.

When I got back to the car after our appointment, there was a bag waiting for me on top of the SUV containing a lavender-scented candle and the sweetest note of encouragement. That unexpected gift quite literally brightened my life—exactly what I needed to carry me through an otherwise hard and lonely time.

Nothing is as daunting as bringing new life into the world, and ever since that day in the parking lot I have looked for ways to pay it forward with other moms. Mothers have been mothering for thousands of years, but rarely do they do it alone. Sometimes all that's needed is another person reaching out to remind us that we're doing a great job at a really hard thing. ∎

His Turn

HIRO I.

After my father passed away in 2001, my mother came to stay with me every summer in Europe. I would head to Japan in June, accompany my mom on the journey to my home, and then bring her back to Japan in September. For 20 years, we've been doing this so she could avoid suffering through oppressively hot summers.

Over the years, my mother's health began deteriorating to the point where I had to help her wash twice a week. It was sad to realize she needed this sort of help, but I was happy to oblige—to do the same for her as she had done for me as a baby.

One year, when she was 86, she was too tired to walk out of the airport after completing the long journey back to Japan. So, I did the only thing that made sense—I carried my mother on my back. Before I could even think about how I was going to manage our luggage as well, three nearby strangers jumped into action, grabbing our bags to accompany us to the taxis. It made sense that I would have to assist my mother. But I was so moved that others would help me do so. ∎

SPOTLIGHT

The financial aid representative at my college selected me as an in-state resident because my family is Native. Huge difference … huge. —*Misha B.*

Something to Hold

RACHEL W.

My electric blue Nissan Sentra was a terrible car for Minnesota winters. It was so lightweight that I had to fill my back seat and trunk with sandbags to get enough traction to avoid being stuck in a snowbank.

That ridiculous Nissan is what I was driving to a gas station a few blocks from my apartment in the Twin Cities. I was a frequent visitor there; I drove right past it every time I left my place, so I always stopped in for coffee on my way to work or class.

Speaking of which, I was *always* on my way to work or class. I was in graduate school for counseling and art therapy, worked full time as a waitress, and had three different internships. I was exhausted and perpetually grumpy, but kept grinding. As they say, the only way to get to the other side is through.

One day I was standing in the gas station checkout line with a cup of coffee—lost in a maddening mental maze, numbed out by sleep deprivation, and barely keeping it together—when I felt someone tap me on the shoulder. I tensed instantly, not having the bandwidth for conversation with anyone, let alone chitchat with a stranger. When I finally turned around, I was met by a man with a small object in his hand. Instinctively, I held out my palm, within which he dropped a small, round stone. Looking down in confusion, I read a painted word across the surface: *Resilient.*

"Someone gave that to me when I was having a hard time," he told me, smiling. "I don't need it anymore. I think you need it."

How did he know? Speechless, I closed my hand around the

> How did he know? Speechless, I closed my hand around the rock, feeling the weight of it, the smooth, cool surface.

rock, feeling the weight of it, the smooth, cool surface. Tears filled my eyes as I whispered, "Thank you." As he walked away, I felt as though I'd been anchored: my mind no longer racing ahead, but firmly rooted to the present. Now, I had something to hold—and, for the first time in a long time, felt held in return.

I paid for my coffee, got in my car, and cried my whole way to school. That unexpected gesture not only changed my day but also served as a reminder for months to come. I was resilient—strong and solid—like a stone.

I kept that rock in my car for a long time. At the time, it was hard to imagine, but I knew one day I wouldn't need it quite so much—that someone else would need it more. ∎

Life's a Beach

JESSICA C.

I became a single mom just as we emerged from the pandemic in 2021. After so many months enclosed within the four walls of my home, going it alone with two kids under five, I wanted to go to the beach. No, I *needed* to go to the beach—for myself, yes, but also for my kids.

For months, I'd psych myself up—It'll be fantastic!—only to chicken out, daunted by the image of my future self, harried, wind-blown, wrangling two kids and a mountain of beach supplies. How would I carry it all? Finally, one day in July, I decided it was time to ignore my self-doubt and just *go*. I grabbed the kids, bundled up our Oregon Trail amount of gear, and headed out the door.

It turned out to be a glorious day. We dipped our toes in the surf, built sandcastles, and splashed in puddles far from the lapping waves. Even the sand that somehow crept into our sandwiches tasted good.

We ended the day inventing weird crab races, circling each other on all fours, rolling around and squealing. Our love felt limitless.

Still, as we packed up to leave—a bag on each shoulder, stroller in one hand, son on my hip, daughter tottering behind—my self-doubt began to return. If only it were possible to give my kids days

like this every day, I thought. But it wasn't. I was a single parent—and a human being. My love may be limitless, but my patience? My energy? My parenting savvy? *Definitely not.* As the critical voice in my head grew louder, threatening to ruin an otherwise perfect day, I heard a woman call out behind me.

"Excuse me," she said. "Miss?"

I was certain I'd dropped something. A ball, maybe. Or a shoe?

"Your family is so beautiful," the woman said. "You're doing a great job."

It was so completely out of the blue, I couldn't believe it. I felt as though I had dropped something—my confidence—and she picked it up, chased me down, and returned it to my hands. She witnessed something precious between me and my kids and wanted to make sure I didn't forget it. That I didn't leave it behind.

On the way home, with the woman's words fresh in my mind, I broke open the lollipops. It felt important, somehow, to honor the day—and to toast our success as our own, unique family. ∎

Invisible Thread

JENNIFER P.

I've tripped a bunch of times in my life, but never as spectacularly as I did the day I tumbled down a flight of stairs at my community college.

Peeling myself from the ground, I looked around, stunned and embarrassed, registering the battalion of shocked faces around me. I assured them I was fine, ha ha, and began to search for my water bottle. The little traitor had compounded my mortification by falling from my bag and clanging loudly downstairs, fleeing the scene. I spotted it, finally, close to the Converse-clad feet of a young man sitting alone at an outdoor table.

I descended the remaining steps with the caution of a land mine defuser, scooped up the bottle, then asked the young man if he wouldn't mind if I sat for a moment, desperately needing to regroup. He nodded. A self-deprecating joke about my clumsiness produced a small smile, but that was it.

I chalk it up to being a mom, which, I think, honed my radar for detecting the difference between a young person who wants to be left alone and one who secretly needs to talk. I sensed he was the latter, but, of course, couldn't be sure. We chatted briefly about our studies—he was an English major; I was an aspiring high school history teacher. I asked if he was excited for spring break—a fairly neutral question, I thought.

"Am I excited for spring break?" he repeated with all the joie de vivre of Hamlet contemplating a skull. Uh-oh, I thought. Had I already committed my second gaffe of the day?

Quietly, he shared that his sister had committed suicide last year—that he was dreading the holiday, with its requisite family visit, which would reinforce his loss. Something about the way he looked at his hands when he spoke made me realize that he felt alone, banished to an island of pain "normal" people can't understand. When he finally met my gaze, I looked him dead in the eye and told him I understood—I'd lived through it, too.

My mother died from suicide before her hair turned gray. She only had the opportunity to hold one of her (now five!) grandchildren. She'd had a whole life in front of her she chose to extinguish—something my sister and I still struggle to accept.

When you lose a loved one this way, it cuts differently from any other type of death. This young man and I belong to a club no one wants to join. But there is some solace in the fact that it is, after all, a club—on this island, where no one's alone and no one's "abnormal."

This was something I yearned to impress upon him while we sat together at that table, surrounded by an ocean called grief. I didn't sugarcoat the truth; that kind of sugar turns bitter in the minds of the bereaved. Life for him would never be the same. Still, loss is change. And change is growth. And growth is good—even if there's pain.

We spoke until it was time for our next class. I watched his demeanor change as he opened up about his sister. It was humbling to be on the receiving end of so much recollected love, to provide a safe ear to someone vulnerable.

Still, as much as I may have helped him that day, he helped me, too, proving to me once more how my mother's suicide—a deep and awful severing—had nevertheless paved the way to human connection.

The young man and I didn't exchange names or contact information, and I haven't seen him since. Still, often when I'm going up stairs, I wonder how he's doing, and whether he remembers our conversation as tenderly as I do. Our commiserated experience of hurt, darkness, and pain moved me beyond words, and led me to believe seemingly random interactions are destined—that lives are, in fact, intertwined.

Perhaps, that day, I didn't fall down by accident. Perhaps I tripped over an invisible thread—the one that connects us all. ∎

Sill de Cuisine

STEFANIA O.

Cooking for only my boyfriend and me can be a struggle, since I always make way more food than necessary. Which is how I became that neighbor who knocks on your door with fresh cookies—the one who checks in.

Ray was one of these neighbors. At first, we'd just smile and say hi. Then, when we had a power outage, we touched base to make sure everything was all right. It wasn't long before my containers of food found their way to him and his wife. But I never expected Ray to reciprocate. When he did, magic happened.

The windows of our adjacent apartments both overlooked the courtyard, each sporting sills large enough to support containers of food. One day I left a gift of candy, and Ray responded with a bottle of wine. Then candy and wine evolved into doughnuts and pasta

and increasingly impressive offerings—I once received a $90 steak! Our windowsills evolved from being mere ledges to our favorite new restaurant: a hip new pop-up with standing reservations for two. We called it the Sill de Cuisine.

Then, COVID came along, closing down restaurants and cafés. But not the Sill. I presented a sweet-and-savory strawberry risotto. Ray took my risotto and raised me matzo ball soup. The culinary hits kept coming, each delicious dish outdoing the last. Cooking for each other became a creative outlet, and our daily delights were a surprising antidote to the dull monotony of lockdown—quite simply, something to look forward to. Each time I tasted a new treat, I felt so cared for—so nourished, in both body and soul. And I knew Ray felt the same way.

> Our windowsills evolved from being mere ledges to our favorite new restaurant: a hip new pop-up with standing reservations for two.

But all good (and bad) things come to an end. I was moving out, and the Sill de Cuisine's days were numbered. The day of my open house, Ray came to the viewing in secret—officially the first time he'd seen the inside of my apartment. I came home to discover steak and pierogi, both from a place he loved, waiting for me in the fridge. He'd left them there as a last goodbye—a final tribute to our unique dining club, and friendship.

Despite having moved out, Ray and I remain good friends. Sometimes, when life feels precarious (as it often does these days), I recall our Sill de Cuisine and remember: Society can shut down, restaurants can shutter. But our hearts, if we choose, can always stay open. No reservations needed. ▪

CHAPTER FOUR

The Kids Are All Right

The future is in great hands

A Modern Fairy Tale

KELLY K.

I gazed up at the ceiling fan, watching the blades spin round and round as I stroked Nova's furry belly, which rumbled with purrs of contentment. At least one of us was happy.

Sometimes, if you stare at something long enough, shapes begin to form. Since the pandemic arrived in Los Angeles, I'd managed to find a rabbit face on my bedroom ceiling, as well as a giant outline of a giraffe. Maybe the universe was telling me that it was time to take a break from playing Animal Crossing.

Glancing over at the clock, I decided it was late enough to venture outside; I couldn't take being cooped up in here one more minute. I scooped up Nova and put her inside a kitty backpack before quietly slipping out the front door.

Nasty breakups are never fun, especially if you're living together. But disentangling myself from my ex while in the middle of lockdown was absolute hell. I stayed in my bedroom all day to avoid him, and at night I went out for long walks or scooter rides to get some fresh air. Normally when I'm depressed or struggling, I go to the gym as much as possible and distract myself with work and my friends. But because of the pandemic, none of that was possible. For now, Nova and I were stuck.

> I had magic to create for a little girl who was lonely in lockdown, and my life started to have color once again.

Walking up and down the hills in the neighborhood kept my body and mind busy. I was so focused on keeping my feet moving that at first I didn't notice what appeared to be a magical fairy garden nestled around a tree planted next to the sidewalk. It had a tiny door on the side of the tree, brightly painted rocks, figurines, and flowers carefully placed just so among the moss and mushrooms. Above all of this, higher up on the tree, was a laminated note that read:

Our four-year-old girl made this to brighten your day
Please add to the magic, but don't take away
These days can be hard, but we're in this together
So enjoy our fairy garden and some nicer weather

These were my people.

Suddenly, I didn't feel so lonely anymore; whatever this was looked like great fun, and I definitely wanted to be involved.

I hurried home, creativity firing on all cylinders. The snide comment my ex threw at me when I walked in the door barely registered; I was on a mission! I had magic to create for a little girl who was lonely in lockdown, and my life started to have color once again.

Four years old is such a transformative age, and I'd thought a lot about how all this isolation was affecting families with young children. I couldn't imagine having to balance working from home and caring for kids. After giving it some thought, I decided to become a fairy named Sapphire. I would be a fun distraction for this little girl and give her something to look forward to.

The next day, I returned to the garden and left a little note to her, introducing myself and letting her know that I had come to live in the tree.

She had set it up so nicely, I wrote, that I simply had to move in! I also told her I would bestow her with a gift of magical fairy dice if she did the following things:

1. Say five nice things to people you love;
2. Do three helpful things for someone in need;
3. Promise to always be kind and brave and show love to those in need; and
4. Draw a picture of your favorite animal so I can show the other fairies.

Additionally, so that her parents wouldn't think I was a lunatic, I left my phone number higher up on the tree so they could text me. I wasn't sure if she would respond, but the next night when I went out for my walk, there was a letter for me. I learned that my little four-year-old friend was named Eliana, and at the bottom of her letter she wrote, "I love you, Sapphire."

No one had said they loved me in so long. I sobbed, right there on the sidewalk. I thought I was saving this little girl from sadness and despair, but maybe she was the one who was saving me.

Eliana earned her magical fairy dice, of course, and we continued to write to each other every day for months, even after I moved to a new apartment. I became so close to her parents that they feel like family. Eliana still thinks I'm a fairy, and we mail each other letters and packages. It's truly the most fun I've had in a long, long time.

I started all of this by trying to create magic for a little girl. But in the end, she created it for me. Because of Eliana, I found myself again. She reminded me that there is never a bad time to sprinkle a little fairy dust, no matter where you are. ∎

SPOTLIGHT

I was playing music for a group of eight-year-olds. One said, "I love this song; it makes me feel like I'm four again." —*Rachel H.*

Enough Said

GERRY M.

I realize I'm far from objective—fine, I'm 100 percent biased. But my daughter Mina is the cutest little girl in the whole wide world. The day she was born, I took one look at her wide eyes and dimpled cheeks, her little face framed by dark brown curls, and thought to myself, Yep, this is perfection. And when Mina had to get corrective lenses a few months later, let me tell you: Those tiny round spectacles only ramped up the cuteness.

When she was two years old and learning to talk, Mina never said much; if something could be expressed in one or two words, she'd do so, boiling it down to the bare-bones basics despite our encouragement to continue. She either didn't want to or didn't need to say more. And either way, I loved it.

> Whenever she was happy, she'd just shout out, "HAPPY!" I'm telling you, there is nothing purer in this world than seeing your baby occupied with toys or studiously munching her toast and then suddenly bursting out that word.

Whenever she was happy, she'd just shout out, "HAPPY!" I'm telling you, there is nothing purer in this world than seeing your baby occupied with toys or studiously munching her toast and then suddenly bursting out that word. She'd shout it as punctuation to pretty much any situation she liked, or as a resolute answer to any question on the "How's Mina?" spectrum. Sometimes, she'd be playing by herself in another room, and we'd hear her clear across the house: "HAPPY!"

Now that she's older, and capable of more "sophisticated" conversation, I cherish that side of her, too. Sometimes, when she's prattling away, using all the words she knows and then some, I can still hear her baby voice—"HAPPY!"—bursting straight out of my heart. ∎

Playing House

HOLLY P.

I was a musician living in New York City in my early 20s, renting a house with eight other roommates. Granted, the setup had its perks. An elegant Brooklyn Victorian that had been converted into a music school in its heyday, it came with a Steinway grand piano and some "soundproof" workspaces in the basement. That said, it was still a house with nine musicians, two bathrooms, and one kitchen.

Like so many young people in the Big Apple, I was embarking on my musical journey, and it was an exciting time. But I was also, for lack of a better word, broke, beginning a lifelong student loan repayment, and struggling to pay for the basic costs of living. And all this just so I could go to Tuesday night open mics, fingers crossed that something would come of it.

During my eight years in New York, I was a barista; a waitress at a Vietnamese noodle shop, an Israeli restaurant, and an Irish pub; a representative for a not-for-profit jazz outreach program; a tour guide at Madison Square Garden; a piano teacher at a very strict school in Chinatown; a private vocal coach; and a nanny.

Though I was only ever let go from one job, none of them ever felt quite right. They say, "If the shoe fits," but I think I just made sure that none of them ever did. I didn't want them to. My eye was on the prize—music—but until I could make money with *that* shoe, I worked three jobs at a time for most of my years in the city. Nannying was by far my favorite.

I worked for one family for about six years. I started watching their oldest when she was just 10 months old. By three, she was smart, and funny, with so much personality. She told it to you straight, so you never had to guess; kids can be refreshing like that. One thing she said to me is something that I revisit often.

We were in the common playroom of their Dumbo apartment building. It shared a space with the resident gym and was the backup plan for stormy days. Lined with buckets of toys and books, it had as its centerpiece one of those Little Tikes plastic houses. I made myself into a wallflower as she explored the room—but I knew I wasn't off the hook.

"Holly [or more accurately, Howwy!], come on! Get in the house!" she commanded. I replied, "Oh, thank you for the invite, but I'm afraid I'm too big for that house."

Her wiggly, silly, three-year-old stance turned suddenly still and contemplative. She looked me square in the eye and walked over to me slowly, with intention. When she arrived, she put her hand on my shoulder and said, "No, Holly. You aren't too big for this house. This house is too small for you." She proceeded to find some other toys we could play with together.

That larger understanding, coming from that tiny human, has always stuck with me. I hope it sticks with her, too. ∎

Snap Judgment

BJ G.

In 1984, at least in my part of the country, boys mostly wore big baseball jerseys and girls tied their hair into high ponytails. Not me. I wore blue jeans, a *Knight Rider* T-shirt, and sunglasses at all times—even indoors. Based on that description, you might think I was the coolest fourth grader in the lunchroom—a regular pint-size Tom Cruise in *Risky Business.* But you'd be wrong.

The cafeteria at school was cacophony central: Utensils clanged, kids chattered, chairs squeaked against the linoleum floor. But it wasn't the sound that bothered me. It was the light. The lunchroom was by far the brightest room in the building, with sunshine flooding in from tall windows and relentless fluorescent ceiling bulbs. To me, bright light was like someone blasting music in my face, refusing to lower the volume.

I was born with congenital myopia and monochromacy (full color blindness), a side effect of which is photosensitivity—basically a fancy term for "light hurts my eyes." To help me cope, my doctor told me to wear sunglasses in all brightly lit spaces—the kind that were round and mirrored, with leather screen protectors on the sides, and an elastic strap around the back of my head. Yeah. Subtle, they were not. Fortunately, I'd attended the same school since kindergarten, so my teachers and classmates were used to my unique appearance. But in the beginning of fourth grade, some new teachers were hired, and one of them—unaware of my medical history—took it upon herself to teach me a lesson.

> I couldn't believe it. Instead of laughing, they rallied around me. I'd been mistaken for a rebel—but they were the truly rebellious ones, defending me in the face of potential serious discipline.

I was about to polish off a chicken nugget when she materialized out of nowhere. "You aren't allowed to wear sunglasses in school," she sniped, clearly mistaking me for a rebel—the resident Cafeteria Cool Kid. Well, she wasn't having it—not on her watch. Before I could explain, she reached over to yank them off, but—because of the elastic—the glasses snapped back, hitting me in the face. I wasn't sitting with my friends that day, so I just sat there, shocked and embarrassed, holding the part of my cheek where the glasses hit, waiting for everyone at the table to laugh.

"He's color-blind!" one kid cried out.

"He has to wear those," another chimed in.

"The sun hurts his eyes."

"He's allowed to!"

I couldn't believe it. Instead of laughing, they rallied around me. I'd been mistaken for a rebel—but they were the truly rebellious ones, defending me in the face of potential serious discipline, including corporal punishment. They stood up for me all on their own.

To this day, I hold that memory close. Even then, I knew I was always going to face many challenges in life—I was different, and because of that, vulnerable to being misunderstood. But that day, I learned firsthand that for every person who snaps to judgment, there's another who doesn't—someone who approaches differences with curiosity rather than prejudice, and compassion rather than condemnation.

Looking back on my life, I see that lesson has been tested, but never broken—and years later, it remains beautifully true. Just as that teacher showed me that blindness has nothing to do with your eyes, those students showed me that kindness is the only way to see. ∎

SPOTLIGHT

I really love Daddy. Where did we get him? —*Lindsay Y.*

From the Mouths of Babes

DAN L.

I magine a building on the side of a hill in Los Angeles—a structure straight out of *Lord of the Rings.* Inside this Hollywood hobbit house are rooms with hidden nooks and crannies, oddly placed doors and stairs. The building floods with light, and when the windows are open, a breeze comes off the ocean. Its last, and most important, attribute: It's a school for young kids.

The whimsical nature of the space lent itself to learning. Up some stairs, within a somewhat secluded wing, was the math classroom, a giant space with huge windows as well as walls with whiteboard paint. We called it the Loft.

This is where I taught.

One day, I was chatting with a nine-year-old student between classes when we noticed the time: We were going to be late! As we bolted upstairs to beat the bell, my student shouted, "It's a race!" Happy to play along, I replied, "Slow down, I'm too old for a race!" To which he cheerfully replied, "Oh, no you're not, you're *hardly* even balding!"

The student was far too young to understand the discomfort their compliment may have caused (because, you know, I *was* hardly even balding!). Today, though, I look back and laugh. Nothing quite matches the honesty and innocence of youth. ▪

> Nothing quite matches the honesty and innocence of youth.

The Benefit of the Doubt

MELYNA I.

At age three, our daughter began dancing with Ballet Lubbock in West Texas. Watching her transform over the years filled me with joy, and once she turned six, I eagerly anticipated her debut in one of ballet's favorite traditions: the annual *Nutcracker* performance. For one of the show's big scenes, my daughter was cast as a snow angel, moving in circular rotations around the stage to simulate a big flurry.

As she ran onstage with the other dancers, my daughter tripped on her skirt, landing face-first. *Splat!* She quickly gathered herself and continued to dance, but tripped again before finally exiting the scene. I held my breath for what felt like an eternity as I walked to the back hallway to greet her and the rest of the group.

We lingered after the other girls left, and she finally let it all out, sobbing as I held her tightly. Once she felt OK again, we joined the audience to watch the rest of the show. I pointed out mistakes even older dancers made in later scenes, and she began to understand she wasn't alone. As we left, I reminded her that mistakes don't taint the big picture of a performance; in fact, they often create space to allow your true colors to shine.

But once we got home, she was met again by another wave of sadness. So, I brought up my experience as a young musician, when my stage fright caused my guitar to quake off my lap, making singing and playing virtually impossible. Once my daughter had finished giggling, I told her that moments like that, embarrassing as they were, ultimately made me a stronger performer. Because mistakes teach us the lessons we need to become better.

By call time the following night, my daughter was bright with renewed energy and confidence. That night, I was one of the mom monitors, backstage with the group. My daughter folded into herself. "I can't do it," she mouthed. In seconds, she was surrounded by a handful of girls; one was holding her gently by the shoulders and looking into her eyes. Without disrupting the moment, I approached and nearly bawled when I heard what they were saying.

"We all fall down sometimes," the other girl told my daughter. "All you need to do is get back up and keep trying. You're not alone. We all do it! We will all be there together." It was simpler than anything I'd told her yesterday, but it was all she really needed to hear.

The routine went flawlessly that night. When the snow angels returned from the stage, the first thing I saw was my daughter's glowing smile. She actually skipped toward me. I can't imagine her feeling quite so joyful if she hadn't tripped to begin with. Because it's one thing to triumph over a routine. It's another to triumph over self-doubt. ∎

World Class

ACHINI P.

When I first got to Poland, it was the apple trees that stood out. They were everywhere, looking for all the world like an ordinary sight. But to me, they were anything but, because we don't have apple trees in Sri Lanka. There, apples are found in the supermarket, not on the side of the road.

It was 2016. I was in the midst of my university studies, and I was in a bad place in my life. So I took a gap year and ended up in Poland, teaching in a primary school as part of a cultural exchange program. The children in my class were between seven and nine years old, and they were so excited to meet me. They'd never met a Sri Lankan before.

"Do you have McDonald's there?"

"Do you live in a forest?"

They had so many questions that I made a presentation with photos of my house, my family, of me eating—yes—in McDonald's. The children were amazed.

> Their curiosity was like rain in the summer heat.

"But you live on an island! You have McDonald's on an island?"

Their curiosity was like rain in the summer heat. I'd never seen such unadulterated, open, beautiful curiosity before. They wanted to know everything, finding particular wonder in the coconut trees. A coconut tree. Who would have thought? They were the apples of Sri Lanka—an ordinary sight, a staple I'd never thought twice about. And yet the children were bursting at the seams with their questions. They wanted to know everything we did with the coconuts.

My favorite part, though, was teaching them about religion. The children surprised me with how much they knew. Buddhism,

Catholicism, Sikhism, Islam, too. I never imagined children could be so knowledgeable—and better still, that they could be so interested.

For once, I saw how different life could be: That schools do not have to be segregated by religion, taught only by staff of the same faith. That children do not have to be beaten to make them listen (corporal punishment is still ingrained in the school systems in Sri Lanka). I watched in amazement as Polish teachers broke up fights by putting children on opposite sides of the room, and once they'd calmed down, bringing them back together to talk.

My entire world had opened up. Sri Lanka is in the throes of economic collapse, all of which can be traced back to the animosity between the religious ethnic groups. If only we were not separated by our faiths, not ignorant of one another. If only we could be genuinely curious about each other, as these beautiful Polish children were about me. If only Sri Lanka could be a more open-minded place.

But as much as I taught my children about Sri Lanka—about me and my religion—the children taught me far more. They showed me that diversity is possible. Acceptance is possible. Unity is possible. I was there only two months, but I am forever changed.

Dare I believe and dream for Sri Lanka? Children, I decided, are the key. In 2018, I pursued my teaching diploma and qualified as a teacher because—yes, yes, I dare to dream. ∎

SPOTLIGHT

When my daughter was about five, I asked her how so many Cheerios got on the floor, and she said, "Gravity." —*Aimee H.*

To Each Their Own

HANNAH F.

Whatever stereotypes arise when you hear the phrase "small town," I'm pretty sure that Laramie, Wyoming, fits the bill. A tiny hub of outsize contradictions—love and hate, beauty and bigotry, wide-open plains and closed minds—Laramie managed to bear witness to the first woman to cast a vote in a United States general election. It was also the site of Matthew Shepard's murder, a hate crime so brutal and shocking it reverberates to this day.

I moved to Laramie to go to the University of Wyoming. But I grew up nearby, in Cheyenne, so it wasn't exactly a culture shock. Whatever distances I'd travel would have to happen internally. To fully appreciate the scope of this journey, please consider the fact that, before college, "gay" was merely something I'd heard of—as if "Gay" were some obscure klezmer band from Iceland, and not, you know, a good 10 percent of the country. As for transgender—totally off my radar. The term, let alone the concept, remained foreign to me until I attended an LGBTQ+ rights symposium, and then it was like: mind blown.

Anyway, it wasn't all symposia and earth-shattering epiphanies that year. I also had a day job, nannying four kids, to pay the bills. While college occupied my head, nannying—one little girl in particular—kept me on my toes.

Brynn was the kind of quick-witted 10-year-old who, through the sheer power of her precociousness, rendered many adults slack-jawed. Between the two of us, she was indisputably cooler, always ready with a crackling insult or the perfect burn. (My retort, if I had one, always arrived a good 24 hours later.) Still, whatever I lacked in wit, I made up for in wisdom—or so I thought.

Once a month, I'd take Brynn with me to a local coffee shop owned by my landlord—it was an easy and fun way to drop off a rent check. I'd order a coffee for myself and an Italian soda for her. Then we'd find a table and people-watch for an hour. During one of these excursions, Brynn locked in on a woman who was clearly transitioning, wearing a neon pink shirt with a green zebra-print skirt—sort of the sartorial equivalent of a Jolly Rancher safari. Brynn took a long sip of soda, frowning over her straw.

"Why does that person look like that?"

I gotta say, for a kid in jean shorts and a University of Wyoming T-shirt, her clutching-her-pearls delivery was A+. Meanwhile, I'm breaking a sweat, like, OK, how do I answer this? I always took care not to express political opinions around the kids—I didn't know their parents' beliefs, for one, and certainly didn't want to cause offense or confusion. Second, being transgender was something I only just learned about in college, right? Exactly how was I supposed to explain this to a 10-year-old?

After a pause worthy of paramedical intervention, I stammered out the most generic, baby-step explanation I could possibly muster. "Um … well … sometimes," I began, forceful right out of the gate, "a person is born in a body that doesn't match who they are inside."

Brynn stopped me with a look, like, Are you kidding me? "I know *that*," she said witheringly. "But why is she wearing that outfit?"

My jaw dropped a little. OK—that's a twist. Here I was, on this laborious trek toward enlightenment—wheezing, stumbling over obstacles, battling biases, and attempting to explain this wild new terrain to a child—only to discover that not only does the kid already know the terrain, the kid was freaking born here. Like so many of her peers, she's waiting on the tallest mountain peak, sipping her soda, tapping her foot—like, What in the world is taking adults so long? It gave me hope for the future. What can I say?

As for the outfit, I told her: to each their own. ∎

A Different Outlook

SPENCER B.

I'm a physical education teacher, and on occasion, I get the opportunity to oversee summer school classes. Let me tell you: Nothing is more exciting than guiding a bunch of seventh graders through physical education exercises when they would rather be at home playing video games or at the swimming pool with their friends. But we have fun (really).

Classes are a little more relaxed in the summer, so I usually begin each day with an organized cardio game like tag or sharks and minnows before splitting the kids into groups to play basketball or volleyball.

One year, a student in my class had some unique challenges,

including a prosthetic leg. After noticing him struggling to keep up, I pulled him aside and encouraged him to take breaks as often as needed, and let him know that in the running games, he wasn't required to actually run unless he wanted to. He insisted on doing so no matter what, albeit at a much slower pace than his peers. It was clear he wanted to be treated like everyone else; he didn't want any special rules. I took note of that and kept a distant but watchful eye.

During summer school, kids from all over the district are brought to one central location, and making new friends can be a challenge. I wasn't sure how other kids were treating him, especially because he was different, so imagine my delight when about a week into summer school, he arrived to class chatting and joking with two other boys. Later that day, the three of them played a game of basketball; he scored on his friends, and they cheered him on, high-fived him. They made sure he had his chances at the basket, and he had such a big smile on his face. In fact, they all did.

> Watching them was like seeing compounding happiness: They simply helped each other have better days through friendship.

The three of them remained close friends for the rest of the summer; I always saw them laughing and smiling in the hallways. Watching them was like seeing compounding happiness: They simply helped each other have better days through friendship. It was just really cool to me.

These days, I think young adults and kids are less prone to excluding people based on "differences" than we often give them credit for. The world has a million problems adults are constantly trying to fix, but kids obviously have something figured out. Maybe we have something to learn from them. I do every day. ■

SPOTLIGHT

My four-year-old asked me to get her a blue crayon. I told her that I was busy cooking dinner, and she could hop up and get the crayon herself. She sighed and said, "Mom, I love you, but I'm busier than you." —*Kristen B.*

It Takes Two

GABRIELA M.

L ast summer, my husband and I took our almost three-year-old
son to an outdoor festival. It had a kid zone with a bouncy castle slide—the sort of thing that's really eye-catching to kids. My son
really wanted to go, and although it was pretty high, it looked safe.
So, I figured, why not?

After waiting patiently in line, his turn finally arrived. But before
he could mount the steps, the adult volunteer in charge of letting
kids on and off stopped him, commenting on how little he was. My
son would probably get scared, she warned; most likely, I'd have to
go up there and rescue him. Still, she grudgingly concluded, I was
the parent and it was ultimately my decision.

The exchange made me doubt my instincts to support my son—
to encourage him to try something new. But I shook it off. What's
the worst that could happen? He'd get scared and I'd have to go up
the slide myself and take him down on my lap?

Up my son went. But then, at about the halfway point, his
eyes flashed with fear; he realized how high up he was going. He
attempted to turn around, but so many kids were behind him now
that he had nowhere to go but up. When he finally got to the top, I
could tell he was afraid.

Great, I thought. The volunteer was right.

But then, something happened. A young girl, between eight
and 10 years old, noticed my son and saw that he was frightened. I
watched in wonder as she walked over and knelt down to comfort
him. She encouraged him to come down the slide with her, and it
didn't take much. He went down with a huge smile on his face, and
when they reached the bottom, he immediately gushed about how
fun it was—and how he wanted to go again.

I thanked the young girl profusely. Unfortunately, it was so crowded I couldn't find her parents to thank them for raising such a thoughtful child who not only noticed that a little boy was scared, but also had the compassion to help him.

It's so hard as a parent, determining when to let your kids take confidence-building risks, and when to protect them. I almost let that volunteer convince me that allowing my son on the ride was a mistake. Instead, it was the best decision I'd made that day. Not only had he confronted his fear and had fun, but thanks to that incredible little girl, he also learned the world isn't necessarily a scary place.

Kindness is there when you need it. ∎

Queens of
Hearts

MABEL A.

It was my first prom as a teacher. Teenagers swanned into the lobby of a local hotel, trussed up like presents, making their way down a red-carpet entry to a formal sit-down meal. In their ball gowns and tuxedos, the boys and girls giggled arm in arm, arriving to the most anticipated event of the year. Among them, one couple stood out: Jenny and Kate.

They were a sweet pair, straight A students, occasionally awkward, always hardworking. Jenny wore glasses, addressing a significant visual impairment that transformed seemingly simple things, like getting around school, into an ordeal. Because bright lights and stairs overwhelmed, Kate squired Jenny to classes, acting as her support. Prom, with its dimmed lighting and strobing disco ball, didn't

strike me as Jenny's cup of tea, so it surprised me to learn Kate had convinced her to come.

Kate guided Jenny by the arm to the dance floor, whispering encouragement. She was by her side the entire night. Within the swirling lights, surrounded by fashion and glitter, they danced—laughing quietly in their own world, each other's faces the brightest lights of all. I watched them, mesmerized.

This was a Catholic school, so I was pleasantly surprised to learn they had an LGBT and BAME (Black, Asian, and minority ethnic) society, a diverse student body including different faiths and kids who were openly gay, lesbian, or transgender. Still, I'd be lying if I said there wasn't a popularity hierarchy—these were teenagers, after all—and sometimes "differences" relegated kids to the bottom of the pile.

> I'd underestimated these teenagers, and now—among their thundering applause—my preconceived notions crumbled.

The old adage "Be yourself" is easier said than done.

As the evening progressed, slips of paper began to circulate: time to vote for prom king and queen. Everyone in attendance, including staff, got to vote. I scribbled down my names, wondered briefly who would win, dropped my vote into the collection basket, and let fate take its course.

With a flair for melodrama, the class president took his sweet time counting. The anticipation was palpable, clouding the dance floor like dry ice. It's just a popularity contest, I reminded myself, preemptively dismissive of the results, which I expected to uphold the status quo. Still, as the speeches wrapped up, I found myself enraptured. The head teacher took his stand.

"And this year," he intoned. "As voted by the class of 2021 by both the student body and staff members …"

A pause. A cryptic smile.

"We have two prom queens."

My breath caught. No way.

"Jenny and Kate!"

The hall erupted with raucous screaming and applause. I couldn't believe my ears. There was no question the girls deserved the honor most, but I hadn't expected—in my own prejudice—that anyone noticed them or cared. I'd underestimated these teenagers, and now—among their thundering applause—my preconceived notions crumbled.

The head teacher presented Jenny and Kate with their crowns on the dance floor. Beaming, they took their thrones. My heart flooded with pride. What a gift, I thought, to be a humble subject in this glorious new realm. ∎

SPOTLIGHT

A kid waddling after a pigeon yelling, "Come here, street chicken!"
—*Emily F.*

Baby Dada

DANNY M.

I'm not breaking any news here, but being a new parent is an exhausting, often tedious endeavor. Just getting through the day feels like a massive victory.

To add to the fatigue, my wife and I tried to do everything by the books with our new son, Theo; we wanted to wait at least a couple of years before completely screwing him up. Part of this attempt at perfect parenting involved limiting his screen time. After all, we didn't want to raise some couch potato who slowly had his brain turned to mush. Homer Simpson, Jr., sounds funnier on paper than it does in practice.

But by the time Theo was around 14 months old, we were so tired—so in need of a break—that we threw in the towel and started letting him watch a little bit of TV. We began with *Mickey Mouse Clubhouse,* then moved to *Sesame Street,* then to that delightful Australian cartoon *Bluey.*

But when those morphed from being a nice distraction to annoying, we searched for something new. Eventually, we settled on the Disney animated action-adventure musical *Moana.*

And my god, Theo adored it. All the songs. The dancing. The beautiful, oceanic setting. Dwayne "The Rock" Johnson's goofball vocal performance as the demigod Maui. The fight scenes with those ferocious coconut pirates the Kakamora. He loved it all.

He was such a fan that *"Mo-na"* (baby talk for *"Moana"*) was one of his first words, appearing in his lexicon shortly after "Mama" and "Dada." *Moana* dolls, stickers, and coloring books began to populate our house.

Theo's an early riser, often getting up around five in the morning just to make my life even more hellish. We had also made the parenting mistake of letting him sleep in bed with us. So at the crack of each dawn, he'd smack me on the forehead, prompting me to roll out of bed and sleepwalk to the living room. Then he would point at the TV and say his first words of the day: *"Mo-na,* Dada, *Mo-na."*

As Theo's happy face glowed blue from the pristine animated Pacific Ocean, I sat on the couch next to him, a *Moana* sticker stuck to my sweatpants, shocked that this was now my life.

Soon, Theo's obsession with *Moana* wasn't limited to just the wee hours of the morning. When there was a lull in any day, he'd look up to me with his puppy dog eyes and say, *"Mo-na,* Dada, *Mo-na,"* prompting me to fire it up.

Moana has wonderful messages about family, redemption, and discovering your place in the world. "It could be worse. He could be into Cocomelon," I joked to my wife. But despite being a top-notch kids' movie, we were still getting sick of it.

I started to look for alternatives, and eventually found a box of old DVDs featuring digitized home videos from my childhood. My aunt Diane had sent them when my dad passed away after a short and horrific battle with ALS, wanting me to have as many memories of him as possible. The DVDs contained clips from my first birthday, my first time playing miniature golf, a few family Christmases and Thanksgivings, and a longer video of my cousins and me at Alcova Reservoir in Wyoming, riding around on boats and bouncing on trampolines.

When I slid one of the DVDs into the player, I was expecting Theo to look at the grainy footage from the 1980s and angrily demand, *"Mo-na,* Dada, *Mo-na."*

But instead, he quietly sat and watched every second of every clip like it was *Moana Two.* I'd point to the screen. "That's Baby Dada right there," I'd say when I'd appear. "And that's Dada's dada," I'd explain when my beloved dad made any cameos.

Theo was mesmerized.

After the first couple of viewings, I thought he would lose interest and begin obsessing over something else; after all, he had watched a little bit of *Finding Nemo* and also loved it. But to my surprise, he started waking up every morning, slapping me on the forehead, pulling me into the living room, and saying, "Baby Dada."

I'd put on a DVD. He'd climb into my lap and point to the TV whenever the baby version of me would appear. "Baby Dada," he'd scream, nearly waking our neighbors. "Yeah, that's me," I'd whisper back. "Dada Dada," he'd say when my dad popped into frame.

I was obviously upset that my dad passed away before he met my son. He would've been a wonderful grandpa, bouncing Theo on his knee and making funny faces, all while cracking next-level dad jokes. Anytime we'd experience a landmark moment, like Theo's first steps, I'd look to my wife and wistfully say, "I wish my dad was here to see this."

As Theo's happy face glowed blue from the pristine animated Pacific Ocean, I sat on the couch next to him, a *Moana* sticker stuck to my sweatpants, shocked that this was now my life.

But these DVDs turned into a nice consolation prize. I was beyond happy that Theo was getting to know his grandpa through these clips, even if it wasn't the full, in-person version of him. In those moments it was as if we were all together—three generations of Marshall boys—watching Baby Me smash cake into my face, sharing memories and enjoying one another's company, like a family is supposed to do.

It was beautiful.

The first couple of years of parenting are rough: all work and little reward. But "Baby Dada" was one of those moments that made me realize that it really is all worth it. ∎

SPOTLIGHT

My son telling me that I smell like love.
—*Angela D.*

The Icebox

ANTONIA N.

As a single mum, one of the things that worried me most when my children were small was whether there was enough of me to go around. Of course, there wasn't; I always felt like I could be doing more. After they fell asleep at night and the house was quiet, I would lie awake and wonder if they were truly OK. Were they learning proper manners? Were they keeping up with their schoolwork? And most important, were they kind?

The children and I lived in London, a 12-hour plane flight away from my parents, who ran a farm nursery school on several acres of land in South Africa. They had all manner of geese, horses, dogs, and other wildlife on their property. The children *loved* to visit their granny and grandad. South Africa was a welcome break from our urban life; on Broadacres Farm, it felt like we could breathe.

> The children *loved* to visit their granny and grandad. South Africa was a welcome break from our urban life; on Broadacres Farm, it felt like we could breathe.

The room we always slept in was nicknamed "the icebox" because it was so delightfully cold in there—especially compared with the oppressive heat outside. It was a large, sunken room with big windows overlooking the garden. My mum, Phedre, would always hide little toys and treats under the king-size duvet for the children to find. They loved running into "the icebox" to see how lumpy the bed looked, before squealing and ripping back the covers to see what surprises were underneath.

My parents had a wonderful sense of humor, which I suppose is a requirement for running a successful nursery school! After one of our visits, my daughter drew a picture of my father jumping on the bed in the icebox room with a huge smile on his face, as my mother wagged her finger at him in dismay. It was a startlingly accurate depiction. We mailed the drawing to South Africa, and several weeks later, imagine their excitement when we received a photo of my parents reenacting the drawing! But that's how my parents were—full of fun and laughter, always looking for ways to bring joy to the people they loved.

When my mum was diagnosed with ovarian cancer, the laughter stopped, and our world screeched to a halt. But she was a strong woman, and because it was caught early and aggressively treated, the doctors were confident that she would be OK. And she was, for a while. We had three healthy years with her before the cancer returned—except this time, it was too late.

Her funeral was held in the nursery school gardens. It seemed fitting to celebrate her life, which ended a few days before her 69th birthday, in the place she had devoted herself to. The natural back-drop of flowers and plants was bedecked in colorful balloons and streamers, and everyone in attendance was wearing colorful cloth-

ing. A thousand people showed up—including many of my mother's former students—and posted stories about her on a large board. She was very, very loved, and although my heart was split in two, I was so happy to see how many people she touched before her time came to an end.

My son, who was eight at the time, watched all this unfold with serious eyes.

During the seated portion of the funeral service, Jamie sat perched in my lap, grounding me as I wrapped my arms around his small body. That day, I stayed too busy to think much about what was happening. But that night, after everyone had gone to bed, the sadness was crushing.

I was lying in the bed that my mum always made up for us in "the icebox," unable to sleep, when I felt movement by my feet. I sat up and saw Jamie's angelic face peering at me in the dark.

"What are you doing?" I whispered, concerned, sweeping his dark hair away from his face.

"I'm staying awake in case you wake up feeling really sad and need an emergency hug from me," he whispered back.

As I wrapped him in my arms, it occurred to me that my son just might be the kindest little boy I'd ever met. I fell asleep that night knowing that my mother taught me well. And even though I was raising two children on my own, they were turning out just fine. ∎

Full Circle

McKINLEY W.

Around her fourth birthday, my daughter, Maisie, became aware of death; her class had been studying Dr. Martin Luther King, Jr., and she was fascinated. Our bedtime chats soon revolved around King's life, leading to questions about a time period that was incomprehensible to her. As my husband and I both assumed they would, her questions progressed to the subject of his brutal and devastating death, beginning mostly with "how" and "why," and then turning philosophical, culminating in the inevitable: "Where do we go when we die?"

I remember pausing and taking a deep breath before giving my thoughts on this, because as most parents know, the wrong answer to a question like that at such a young age can cause weeks of nightmares or irrational fears. As Maisie snuggled with her small stuffed penguin, I answered as delicately, yet as matter-of-factly as I could. I told her the truth is we don't know—no one truly knows what happens when you die—but that people have faith in a variety of ideas that help give them peace.

My grandfather was raised by Seventh-day Adventists in a very small and poor town in Illinois during the Great Depression. Certain circumstances of his life—the traumatic aspects of his time in the Air Force while stationed in the Pacific during World War II, his lifelong dedication to self-education—drew him away from organized religion, leading him to reject most beliefs he was taught in childhood.

I remember him sharing his thoughts on death through the framework of physics. Energy can never be destroyed, he explained, and that remained true of the energy we create as humans while we're alive. All the beauty, pain, love, and fear carried within us would be reborn in our world, manifesting as energy within other living things. "After I'm gone," he told me, "look for me in all the beautiful living things in the world."

So, 33 years later—and about 19 years after he died—that's exactly what I told my daughter, adding that this was how my grandfather explained it to me, and that I'd found it comforting, and hoped she did, too. She stared off into space and sucked on her hand, something she does when she's trying to ground herself. Then, silently, she pulled down her unicorn eye mask. We snuggled until she fell asleep.

A few months passed. Signs of spring were finally appearing in the Hudson Valley, where we live, and we spent a beautiful April afternoon at a friend's house, playing outside and enjoying the weather. My friend's property includes a stunning pond nestled in a little valley, home to all kinds of life: croaking frogs, budding blooms—and, on this day, a big, bloated dead fish washed up on its bank.

> "After I'm gone," he told me, "look for me in all the beautiful living things in the world."

Maisie immediately ran to sit down beside it, staring blankly. I walked over and crouched beside her, offering all the normal platitudes about the cycle of life, and pointing out that the fish's big size meant it had probably lived a long and peaceful life in that very nice pond. My daughter, who almost always has something to say, was quiet. When I told her I was here to talk about it if she wanted to, she sat for another moment and then, without a word, jumped up to play with her friends.

A few hours later, as we walked over to the car to head home, a butterfly fluttered by and landed on the car door. Anyone from the Hudson Valley will tell you a butterfly in mid-April is a rare occurrence. So, we all took notice.

"Mom, look!" my daughter said. "It's the dead fish."

Her words wrenched at my heart. She didn't know this but, while she and the other kids played, the other parents and I talked about a recent school shooting—in Nashville, close to where I grew up in Tennessee. My sense of helplessness and fear were still so close to the surface that when she made this connection—the fish to the butterfly—I broke into tears. Kneeling down, I gave her a long hug, squishing her against me, wishing I could just put her back into my body and keep her safe forever.

That night I thought about my grandfather—about all the pain and love and beauty he experienced in his life, that no one else will ever know. In that moment, with my daughter, all those years later, I felt them so intensely. ∎

SPOTLIGHT

Baby sister, age five: We were watching an older black-and-white film on Christmas. There was a scene with a horse and wagon and I was explaining that's how people used to travel. Then I said, "Aren't we so lucky to have cars now?" And she said, "Yeah, and I'm glad we have color now, too." —*Chris Y.*

CHAPTER FIVE

When I Needed It Most

Love, loss, and everything in between

Urgent Care

SANTIAGO P.

Some moments in life feel so bizarre that you find yourself wondering if you're dreaming. I think that's what people mean by an out-of-body experience.

That's how I felt the day my father almost died.

My parents are immigrants from Mexico, so we grew up in a very different cultural environment. My dad was a factory worker until he retired, logging long hours and returning home exhausted, often too tired to play with me. He may not have shown much physical affection, but he demonstrated his love in other ways, like surprising me at the end of a long day with my favorite dish or sewing up a pair of my ripped uniform pants while everyone else was sleeping.

I could always depend on him to be there for me, no matter what. So the day he was admitted to the hospital without warning is a day I'll never forget. The situation quickly became critical, and he was moved to intensive care. My mother refused to leave his side. When his heart rate began to drop, I stood there, frozen, as doctors and nurses did everything they could to save him.

The medical team deluged my mother with questions about his medications she couldn't answer, so she begged me to hurry home and get the paperwork the doctors had requested. In a panic, I raced from the hospital and frantically flagged down a taxi. It was raining—the hardest rain in Southern California I could recall. Almost instantly, water soaked through my clothes and shoes. The driver, dressed in a black hoodie, turned around to ask where I was headed, and from the expression on my face, intuited immediately this was a life-or-death situation.

That guy—bless him—drove like a bat out of hell. We weaved in and out of traffic, tires screeching when he whipped into my parents' driveway. He waited for me while I ran inside and grabbed the papers, then drove equally fast to get me back to the hospital. When we came to a rolling stop in front of the double doors, he told me not to worry about the fee.

"Just go in there and save your dad."

Because of how quickly I was able to return with my father's health history, the doctors were able to determine the source of the problem and addressed it immediately. If I'd gotten there even a few minutes later, it's possible he wouldn't have made it.

I feel incredibly fortunate to have my dad in my life today. I no longer take his presence for granted, and I owe it all to a stranger in a black hoodie, who treated my life-and-death situation as seriously as he would his own. ▪

Rent Control

ALEXIS P.

Grief is such a complicated thing. When someone close to you dies, everyone else's world keeps turning while yours grinds to a sudden halt. It's like standing still in the middle of a carousel, watching everyone go by.

At least, that's how it felt when my beloved father-in-law died unexpectedly in his sleep. In California, where I live, employers grant up to five days of paid bereavement leave, but my husband and I needed much more time than that. We were grief-stricken and in shock, but still had to go through the motions of parenting our two children, planning a funeral, and keeping our home running. The bills began to pile up, and we knew financial strain would be soon to follow. But each of us was truly doing the best we could to make it through the day without breaking down in tears.

> Grief is such a complicated thing. When someone close to you dies, everyone else's world keeps turning while yours grinds to a sudden halt.

Our home is a rental that we've lived in for about seven years, and we've always had a good, but professional, relationship with our landlord. He's a put-together man who has never been anything but kind to us. We informed him of the death in our family, but we didn't ask for assistance or permission to pay our rent late. Out of the blue, he sent a text to my husband, which my husband then forwarded to me:

Hi Oscar,
I wanted to thank you and your family for being great all these years. I also wanted to send my condolences again for the loss of your father. You have worked hard, and I'd like to show my

appreciation and waive the month of November. I hope this
helps with some Christmas shopping or whatever else it can
help out with. So please, no need to send me November's rent.
We'll pick back up in December. God bless.

I burst into tears, overwhelmed by his generosity and thought-fulness. We were so moved to know that there are people who care and are willing to extend a helping hand without asking for anything in return.

Life has been good to us, though we've suffered many losses. We still have our family, we're still very close, and we're still breathing. There's a lot to be grateful for at the end of it all. ■

SPOTLIGHT

Three years ago, I was having an abortion and I was alone at the clinic. The doctor had just told me I could have an infection. I was in the waiting room, almost crying and very scared. A woman across the room saw me and came over to sit next to me. She told me she was also having an abortion and was also scared. She already had kids, and she didn't want to be a mom of a new baby at her age. She started telling me things, how the process was for her and the sadness and relief that came with the decision. Maybe she doesn't know how much she did for me that day, but man— that woman saved me. Made me feel less alone in a very scary process. —*Estefany G.*

The Front Porch

LYNNE C.

My grandmother's front porch was too small for chairs—it was more of a stoop, really, providing just enough space for her to stand as she waved visitors inside. For as long as I can remember, every time we went to see her, she was already standing outside, a big smile on her face. As we exited the car, she would chirp, "Well, hi!" as though she'd waited all day for that very moment.

My grandma and I were kindred spirits; with her, I always felt understood. I could talk to her about anything, and she never tired of my questions. We baked, I played dress-up with her clothes and jewelry, and she taught me how to squeeze juice from the oranges growing outside.

She was a beautiful woman, and when she died, it felt like a light went out. I wasn't sure what my life would look like without her in it. After her funeral service, I quietly confided in a friend of hers, Fred, that I was really dreading returning to her house. The thought of an empty porch without her there to greet me broke my heart. I didn't want to face it.

Fred listened intently, angling his head toward me to ensure he

caught every word. He wore big glasses that magnified his gentle, twinkly eyes. I knew him well from the work he'd done with my grandma over the years at their church; Fred was a prankster, someone with whom I'd shared many laughs. Talking to him for a few moments brought me a lot of comfort, his presence helping to quell the dread in my stomach.

After the interment, it was time to drive to my grandmother's house and face reality without her. I cry every time at the memory: my growing sadness as we drove up the street, weighing so heavily on my heart, followed by the surprise of seeing the porch not empty, but occupied—by Fred.

He looked at me so tenderly as he opened his arms for a hug. "I didn't want you to come home from the cemetery to an empty porch."

I don't have adequate words to describe the gift Fred gave me that day. True, my grandmother was no longer there to greet me. But everything she embodied—compassion, attunement, sensitivity— lived on through her friend, communicated in one simple gesture.

In that moment, I realized I didn't fear the empty porch so much as an empty heart. Fred filled it that day with love. ∎

A Part of You

JULIAN E.

Cameron and I were randomly paired as freshman roommates. He struck me as a sort of wacky musician/stoner guy, a natural-born extrovert. I was more guarded and introspective, a film student who avoided girls as much as Cam pursued them. Whereas he was bold, uninhibited by social mores, I played my cards closer to the vest. Our opposing personalities seemed built for comical "odd couple" conflict, but we never really clashed. We just didn't click.

So, while Cameron occupied himself with video games and high romance, I poured myself into schoolwork and creative pursuits. My experiences with girls were all sort of drunk and chance and thwarted, driven by what I *should* want, rather than what I did. I told myself I was "asexual," which was simpler than the alternative: admitting that—maybe—I wasn't attracted to women.

This reluctance to "come out"—even to myself—feels strange in retrospect. I knew the people who mattered—my parents and friends—would be accepting. Still, there were others, on the periphery. One of my strongest childhood memories involves an uncle who, after a few beers, opined on the subject of marriage: "You're damned if you do, and you're queer if you don't. And I'd rather be damned than queer."

So, it wasn't until I moved to L.A.—far away from family and friends—that I felt free to reinvent myself. Or, more accurately, disassemble the invention I called a self. This was before apps, so—in the interest of research—I went on Craigslist to check out the gay personal ads. Not to actually *do* anything, I told myself. Just to "rule out the possibility."

I was able to stick to the sidelines, to convince myself I wasn't interested. Until, one day, I came across this guy's profile, and general curiosity gave way to something more specific. Aaron was attractive, and I found what he wrote smart and compelling. I reached out, and we started a sort of pen pal conversation. It was wonderful; I felt seen and real. But when we got to the point where we discussed meeting in person, he dropped a bomb. He had a wife.

At that time, I was 22. I'd spent years consumed by thoughts I didn't allow myself to think, feelings I didn't allow myself to feel. But I don't think I was aware. Not really. Not until I found someone to talk to. The idea of losing that the second I'd found it, of returning to my half-self purgatory: It was too painful. So, I agreed to meet him, "just to continue the conversation."

We met at a frame shop, and I still have this image of us standing in front of the display—this gigantic, empty frame around us. In my memory, it's a snapshot—the moment I emerged from Denial into Truth. It should have been beautiful, but it wasn't. Because the instant I emerged from one secret (my own), I became consumed by another.

> At 22, I'd spent years consumed by thoughts I didn't allow myself to think, feelings I didn't allow myself to feel.

For months, I felt overwhelmed, ricocheting between exhilaration and shame. The highs weren't worth the lows—I knew that. I was hurting his wife, whether or not she knew it, and I was hurting myself, whether or not *I* knew it. But because Aaron was the only person I could talk to—about me, about us—I felt trapped. It was a little like Munchausen syndrome by proxy, in that I kept going back to the person making me feel bad to help me feel better.

Then, one day, in the thick of everything, my old roommate Cameron called. Turns out, like me, Cameron had another side—slower to emerge, a kind of sage, Buddha-esque quality. By the time college ended, we'd actually become good friends. Unlike Aaron, with whom things had developed at a frenzied pace, my friendship with Cam had required time to grow.

Perhaps detecting something was off, he asked me what was going on. I just couldn't keep it in; the entire story came flooding out. At the very end, realizing what I'd just confided, and to *whom* I'd confided—not my secret-life boyfriend, but a real-life friend—I let out a deep sigh. "And that's me," I said. That's how I punctuated the story. That's how I punctuated myself.

He was quiet on the other side of the line, and I braced myself for judgment. But, instead, he said, "That's not you—that's just a part of you."

Somehow, that simple, mantra-like response completely shifted my perspective. Cam didn't give me advice. Instead, he provided a simple recognition that this painful relationship didn't define me, didn't contain all I was.

It wasn't instantaneous, but that marked the beginning of a new phase. I ended the relationship, and credit Cameron's simple mantra for giving me the strength. Gradually, the picture frame within which I'd been constricted fell away: I was more than a moment in time, more than a mistake, more than my fear. I was a whole, complex person. ■

SPOTLIGHT

In Target, I got the call from the hospital telling me about a major surgery my then two-year-old was about to have. I answered all the questions and got the info I needed for the procedure that would happen in about 10 days. After I hung up, I just stood there, kind of frozen. A woman who was in the same aisle had overheard the two-minute call, and had remained there the whole time, just quietly waiting. After I hung up, she waited a moment and then said, "Do you need a hug?" I nodded. She hugged me, and said, "Whatever it is, it will be OK." It was so kind, so loving. I will never forget it. —*Molly L.*

The Right Medicine

KIM R.

Brown's Pharmacy was the oldest drugstore in our small town, locally owned and operated by a man named Harry. If you plopped him in the middle of some other town, he'd probably pass by unnoticed—but here, he was practically famous. Even when he ventured out beyond the pharmacy walls without his telltale white coat, everyone knew and recognized him.

Eventually, franchised pharmacies began popping up on every corner, but we stuck with Harry. Not only did he have excellent prices, but he knew everyone by name. The place was cozy, with a long soda counter where people could sit while their prescriptions were filled. We could look forward to dough-nuts on the counter, coffee brewing in a pot. It felt like home—like we were sitting in a warm kitchen, rather than a store.

Two days before Thanks-giving, my eight-year-old son, Stephen, had a severe asthma attack that nearly took his life. He spent five days in the intensive care unit, and by the time he was released, I was exhausted. I'd held myself together for nearly a week for my family's sake, but as I drove to pick up Stephen's medicine from the pharmacy, I noticed my hands on the wheel were shaking.

As tends to happen in small communities, someone had already informed Harry about my son's situation. As soon as I walked in, he dropped what he was doing to ask how Stephen was feeling. I numbly recited the events of the last few days, holding a stack of prescriptions in my still-shaking hands and trying not to cry. Then Harry looked directly at me and said, "And how are you doing?"

No one had thought to ask me that, and it caught me off guard. My eyes brimmed with tears. Harry gently guided me to a spot at his soda counter and instructed me to have a seat. He selected a lemon-filled doughnut, handed it to me along with a hot cup of tea, and told me to take 20 minutes to myself while he filled our prescriptions. "Just breathe," he called over his shoulder as he walked away.

So I did.

Harry was so much more than a pharmacist. He knew how to take care of people—understood that medicine doesn't always come in the form of pills or tinctures. Sometimes, the medicine we most desperately need is a concerned question, a little time to ourselves, and a doughnut.

I didn't show up with a prescription for compassion—but Harry filled it anyway. ▪

The Perfect Formula

ELIZA M.

My husband and I adopted a newborn in April 2022—right in time for the U.S. baby formula shortage. At the time, our brand-new daughter needed a specific kind, in very short supply, called Enfamil Enspire Gentlease.

Registered, trademarked, and impossible to find.

Enspire Gentlease was the only formula our daughter could take—all the others made her sick. I joined a regional Facebook group where parents snapped photos of shelves at local grocery stores, time-stamping and posting them for others to see. It was an informal way of checking stock without driving to every store in the area. I was impressed by the group, which existed only to help one another.

By mid-May, our situation was getting dire. We were almost completely out of formula for our still very new baby and could not for the life of us find any in stores. I decided to post in the group, explaining my predicament. Shortly after, I got a private message from Katie. Her daughter used the same formula and she empathized, writing, "If I ever find some, I'll buy for you, too."

A few days later, I got a message from Katie saying she'd found a few cans of the rare formula and had bought some for me. She said it was all paid for—all I needed to do was pick it up from the store. I did immediately, but when I asked her what I owed, Katie refused payment. The Enspire line from Enfamil is double the price of typical formula, so I insisted. Again, she refused. I all but cried and thanked her deeply.

A few weeks later, when our supply was running dangerously

low again, Katie messaged me. "There's a store where I can pick up in Michigan—I'll get you some and we can meet up." We lived just north of Cincinnati, Ohio, so it would have been quite a drive for us.

A few hours later, we met in the parking lot of a strip mall. After a big hug, Katie opened the trunk of her car to reveal an entire pallet of formula. My jaw dropped. This amount of formula—easily a two-month supply—was a huge deal.

Katie revealed that her daughter had been born with some medical issues that required her to be on the Enspire Gentlease. "I promised myself," she said, "that when my baby got healthy, I'd do everything possible to help others."

On my drive home with a carful of baby formula, I started crying. My daughter was so little, her digestive system so delicate, and Katie's efforts to locate and transport the formula moved me beyond words. I'm not a religious person, but something about Katie's generosity vaulted her to a special sphere. She was truly an angel on Earth.

A few months later, our daughter was finally able to switch to a more generic form of Gentlease. I made sure to pay it forward, giving away my extra formulas through the group.

If you judge a society by how they treat their most vulnerable, you should look at how a community takes care of its babies. That Facebook group gave me real hope for our future. I don't know how I would have gotten through those early months without them.

Katie, especially. ∎

More Than Meets the Eye

SUSANNE C.

The moment it happened didn't strike me as particularly profound. But it stuck with me, this seemingly insignificant exchange at my optometrist's. So I must have known, deep down, that an extraordinary kindness had taken place.

I was in ninth grade. My mother—long divorced from my father and only recently divorced from my stepfather—had just relocated me and my siblings from our rinky-dink neighborhood in Miami, Florida, to Great Neck, one of the fancier suburbs of New York City.

It was in Great Neck where I first learned we were different—and not in a good way. For lack of a better word, we were poor—at least, compared to the little Rockefellers we went to school with. We qualified for free lunches—which, when you're 14, taste a lot like the last shreds of your dignity slapped between two slices of Wonder Bread. Our clothes were secondhand and not terrific. But the real impoverishment, looking back, had nothing to do with money.

Today, my mom's condition is pretty well understood. Now, there's a diagnosis and a prescribed course of treatment, therapy, support groups, and we at least pay lip service to "removing stigma from mental illness." But back in the 1970s, we just said you were nuts. So, that was my mom: bonkers, batshit, salted by tears, roasted by madness. Nuts.

As a kid, I quickly learned to not rely on my mom for anything. So while she cried in the bathroom for a year, I hardened into what you'd call a tough cookie (nut free). I parented myself (badly), worked a crummy retail job, and pumped gas at two separate gas stations. If I needed to be somewhere, like a school event or party,

I hitchhiked (which even in the '70s was a crazy thing to do). Still, the two risks—possible abduction and murder—paled in comparison to asking my mom for help.

I didn't want to be seen with her. I didn't want to be seen—full stop. But with my discount wardrobe and latchkey looks, I didn't have a choice. In Great Neck, blending in required money, piles of it. So I stuck out—like a hitchhiker's thumb.

It makes sense, in an ironic sort of way, for an aspiring invisible girl to find her hero in an optometrist. He was a young guy—probably in his 20s—sporting wire-rimmed glasses and a Tom Selleck mustache. (Back then, every man 15 and over had to have a Tom Selleck mustache.)

I'd just finished my eye exam. For the bulk of our medical care, we'd depended on the ER, because most doctors refused Medicaid. But the optical shop in Great Neck was an exception. I wandered around, checking out the neatly folded pairs of glasses under glass.

It was my first time picking out a pair by myself, and one in particular entranced me: aviators, shining like they came directly from the set of *Charlie's Angels*. They were so cool—gold-rimmed with a light blue lens—the kind you'd see on Cher or Jane Fonda in a magazine. In those glasses, I knew I'd look totally different—which is to say I'd finally look the same as everyone else. Not the bravest aspiration, maybe, but a typical one for a teenage girl. And an urgent one for a neglected, emotionally abandoned teenage girl like me.

Before I could get too swept up in fantasies of anonymity, a saleswoman interrupted my reverie. "Oh no!" she exclaimed with a note of dismay. "Those aren't covered by your insurance. You have to choose from the ones over here."

She steered me toward another showcase. Inside were glasses so thick and geriatric they evoked Mr. Magoo. I remember looking at them and just thinking, Oh God, that's it. Nothing dramatic. No obvious outward sign of my crumbling inner devastation. Which is why I believed the optometrist when he interrupted to say, "Sorry, we made a mistake."

He took the aviators down from their place on the wall; he must have noticed me eyeballing them before. "Try these on," he said. I did—and suddenly, the phrase "rose-tinted glasses" ceased to have meaning. Nothing struck me as more beautiful than this blue-tinted world.

"Those are included," the optometrist informed me, apologizing again for the mistake. He ordered them for me.

For whatever reason, those glasses not only made me feel like I could belong. They made me feel like I was OK—like it was all going to be OK. There was something magic about them. When I got to school, I felt protected by a force field of confidence.

Many years later, when I looked back on the moment from a greater distance, I finally saw it for what it was. The shop hadn't made a mistake; those glasses were a gift. And I'm sure they weren't cheap, so it would have been an out-of-pocket expense for the business.

Somehow, that optometrist picked up on my disappointment—not only regarding the glasses, but also on my whole situation: my mother, my childhood. He saw me. He could have made a whole production of it, but he just did it. Part of his kindness is that he didn't want me to know. ▪

SPOTLIGHT

Saved me from drowning in a river in 2019. Never saw him again.
Thanks, Jeff! —*René M.*

Taking Life by the Wheel

ROSE MARY S.

You know how you can walk into a room, spot one of those tall-and-handsomes, and your heart just goes, Oooh? That's him—a six-foot-one maintenance guy with blue eyes—sitting at the end of the bar. Turned out, he was a charmer—the type to turn up at your house unannounced to cut the grass for no reason.

He flew into my life like Peter Pan—but let's face it: Peter Pan isn't cut out to be a dad. Unfortunately, I didn't find that out until after I became pregnant.

He promised he'd look after our little family. But night after night, he'd come home drunk, reeking of alcohol. Whatever hope I had vaporized like spilled liquor.

After the inevitable blowout, I ended up staying at his granddad's house—heartbroken, jobless, with a one-year-old. He kept saying he'd come back, and I believed him; the alternative was too painful. We were a family, weren't we?

No. He imploded that fantasy with a single phone call. He just couldn't do it, he said. (Like I could?)

With his deadbeat status official, I knew I'd have to get back into the workforce—do whatever I could to create a better situation in life for my daughter. I asked my ex if he'd watch her so I could go for an interview—no dice. I had no choice but to take my baby with me, which was nerve-racking for multiple reasons. How could I go back to work if I couldn't even find childcare for an interview? But she was a pretty easy kid—I could sit her down and do something, secure in the knowledge she'd still be playing when I got back. Together, we got the job.

It was the break I sorely needed. The money was great and I

worked weekends, leaving the rest of the week to spend time with my daughter. With this job, I could rebuild, start fresh.

But, still, it takes time to get back on your feet. And your feet don't always take you where you need to go. Which is to say, my car needed gas. And that gas cost money. On my way to work, I stopped to fill my tank. But when I swiped my card at the pump, I was declined. Twice. I went to the register—same results. To my horror, I realized I'd miscalculated my funds. I was supposed to be at my shift in 15 minutes and had no one to call. There were people behind me in line, a cashier looking at me, like, Any day now, lady. And, oh God, what about food and rent? Because how would I get into work at all?

I imagined losing my job. I pictured my daughter in front of her toy computer, her sweet grin when she'd say, "Mommy, I'm at my work job!" That's what she called it, her work job. She was pretending to be me—she was proud—and I wanted that to continue. Because no way was "Mommy, I'm in line at unemployment!" a fun game.

> It takes time to get back on your feet. And your feet don't always take you where you need to go. Which is to say, my car needed gas. And that gas cost money.

A middle-aged gentleman with a mustache brushed past me holding out a $20 bill.

"For the lady's tank."

All I could do was thank him. You see things like this in the movies and, sure, you read stories. But when it happens to you, you can't believe it.

Eleven years down the line, I'm still standing—with a husband I can rely on and a home with my name on it. If I've learned one thing, it's the importance of being self-reliant.

Still, life can knock you sideways, and when that happens, a random act of kindness can make all the difference. When that man gave me money for gas, he allowed me, at long last, to take life by the wheel. ∎

Sine Wave

LUCIA K.

The first and last time I did stand-up, a psychiatrist diagnosed me with bipolar II. I was 28, fresh off a breakup, a new resident of Los Angeles, and 100 percent certain I was on the cusp of a budding career in comedy. The plan? One perfectly executed set, seamlessly delivered with the frills, energy, and infectious charisma I exhibited in my everyday life. I'd be whisked off to West L.A. and signed with a major agency immediately. I felt it in my bones.

It was technically an accurate call on the doctor's part, but the delivery could've used some work.

"Some of the greatest artists of our time had bipolar, you know," my psychiatrist said.

"Oh yeah?" I retorted.

"Yes! ... Like van Gogh."

"Oh, the guy that cut his ear off?? Cool."

I sobbed in his office. I became rageful and icy; how dare this man take my childhood dream and twist it into something so deformed? Thanks so much, doctor. I'm good. Fuck you.

Bipolar episodes look like sine waves. First, an exponential curve swings you up into hypomania, the most euphoric high you've ever experienced (without drugs) and then, the crest and fall: You hurtle into a depression that pummels you so hard into the earth, it's impossible to find the sliver of light that'll pull you out of it.

In denial about my diagnosis, I refused treatment and rode my perilous, unmedicated high for months. And let me tell you, it was a *blast*. I was whip-smart. Funny. Quick. "Magnetic," as one person called it. I made friends everywhere I went: had cocktails with the CVS pharmacist, exchanged Instagram handles with the Uber driver. I got four tattoos in a month while dating four people at once. Conversations in the mirror at that time sounded something like, "I think I might be the hottest person in the world … ?" You get the point.

And then … the crash. It started with a slow week at work that should've felt liberating, but instead felt paralyzing. I wasn't getting the attention I deserved. Impostor syndrome spiraled into an endless cycle of intrusive thoughts accosting my sense of self, integrity, and personhood. My brain betrayed me, playing a loud, looping track that bullied me into oblivion: I was pathetic. Weak. Worthless. Had no friends. And no one was coming to save me.

That week turned into months of barely being able to get out of bed, let alone do anything else. Every day I'd count down the minutes until I could go back to sleep to quiet the thoughts. Every morning felt like a rude awakening back into hell.

My sisters, Savannah and Maya, came over and put me on Face-Time with my older brother, Dwight, who lived in Brooklyn and had weathered serious bouts of depression in the past.

"I haven't eaten in two days," I admitted to him.

"Louie, you need to get up. You need to eat. Something small. Anything."

"I don't know how to explain this, but I can't."

"OK, I'm comin'."

"What? No. You don't have to do that."

"I'd like to. See you in eight hours."

Dwight flew from Brooklyn to Los Angeles that day.

For the next six months Dwight and I—a big brother and little sister in our 30s—became roommates.

I took a sabbatical from work and entered a treatment program for people with addiction and mental health issues. I went five days a week for four months. I had five therapists. I can confidently say this was the worst, most painful time of my life.

The "big things" while living with Dwight were lifesaving: breathing exercises for when I'd wake with my heart pounding in terror, constant reassurance when I'd come home from treatment sobbing that this devastating period of life wasn't forever. "I'm proof," he'd say.

But when it came to what actually healed me, it was the little things. Humor. Words of affirmation (for us both). Coffee. Movies (Tarantino). Old *Simpsons* episodes. Encouraging me to dress up as a fried egg for Halloween (I did). Jazz (Robert Glasper). Seltzer. *Love Island* season eight … (Ekin-Su and Davide forever).

Day by day, minute by minute, Dwight helped crack open the light in my brain with the little, understated things that made life worth living. Probably without even realizing it, he hacked away at the debris that had cluttered my mind for six months. I'll never be able to thank him enough.

So the doctor was right: I have bipolar II and I'll have to battle this disorder the rest of my life. But I also know that I have the staunch support of a family that loves me, an army of supportive friends, and lifesaving medication (shout out, lithium).

Thanks to my big brother, I'm buckled in, ready and willing to ride the wave. ∎

SPOTLIGHT

I fainted on a bus once, just as I was about to get off. The driver contacted the depot and said that he didn't think I was fit to walk home, so he asked for permission to take me home. The depot agreed, as long as all the other passengers agreed. They did, and the bus drove me home through very narrow streets with roundabouts. —*Mirella K.*

A Lifetime of Love

MYRA S.

We lost our firstborn daughter, Havi Lev Goldstein, on January 20, 2021, at 9:04 a.m. She died peacefully in our bed, in my arms, from a cruel disease called Tay-Sachs, which over the course of 12 to 18 months strips your mind and body of every function. Havi was two years, four months, and 16 days old when she died.

My husband, Matt, and I underwent genetic testing for Tay-Sachs; we are both Ashkenazi Jews, a population that has a higher risk for the genetic mutation that causes it. We took the testing seriously. My results showed I was a carrier; Matt's showed that he was not. Because both parents need to be carriers for the fetus to be at risk, given the autosomal recessive nature of the disease, it seemed we were in the clear. Months later, we were pregnant with our first child.

Tragically, Matt received the wrong test result, and his status was misreported. Matt was, in fact, a carrier. Fifteen months into Havi's life, we learned that she was now a victim of this fatal, progressive neurodegenerative disease. In an instant, we were transformed from first-time parents to first-time parents of a dying child.

Ten days after Havi's devastating diagnosis, an extraordinary couple pulled us across the threshold of uncertainty and fear into their honest and love-filled home. Twenty years earlier, Blyth and Charlie's middle daughter, Cameron, also died of Tay-Sachs. They were us, but on the other side of that threshold.

After we adults took turns hugging, Blyth and Charlie reached for Havi, taking turns holding her with unselfconscious warmth.

From then on, they became irreplaceable, cherished guides in our lives and the unconscionable journey of grieving.

Blyth and Charlie live what they know to their core: You can't "fix" devastating loss. Each day since her death, they invite Cameron into their lives, realizing the power of her presence. Bearing witness, time and again, helps buoy them through their lifelong journey with grief.

Our friends take heightened pleasure in the good and the beautiful, and have brought this active consciousness to us. In one ritual, they share a poem with us every Wednesday, because Havi died on a Wednesday, and it is holy to us. Fifty-two thoughtfully chosen poems a year capture and hold our daughter's essence.

> We found moments of beauty and celebration embedded in our deepest pain. And we treated every moment as sacred, not scary. As holy, not superficial.

Every Friday night, we honor Havi's life with family and friends in a celebration that we call Shabbirthday. A combination of "Shabbat" and "birthday," the occasion features challah, the delicious braided Jewish bread that we eat every Shabbat and Havi's favorite food. And because she only had two birthdays, we threw her 57 Shabbirthdays before she died. Balloons, cakes, beach walks, fancy dinners, always a challah, and beautiful songs and prayers.

We didn't pretend to be happy on these Shabbirthdays; we were heartbroken. But we didn't throw parties to distract or numb the pain. Instead, we found moments of beauty and celebration embedded in our deepest pain. And we treated every moment as sacred, not scary. As holy, not superficial.

So how do we characterize a life-changing relationship? First, it is life-sustaining, one that makes all the sense in the world and none at all. Charlie and Blyth offer us marital advice by sharing their own blessings and bruises. They share their oldest daughter, Taylor, and their youngest, Eliza, with us—and through them, we imagine multiple generations of love and connection with our own two living children, Kaia and Ezra. Charlie and Blyth invite us for dinner, to laugh and cry or just be quiet, comfortable in our shared knowingness.

From the date of Havi's diagnosis—December 17, 2019—to her death on January 20, 2021, we followed her lead. She never spoke a word, never walked a single step. But she communicated powerfully through smiles and tears, through the brightness of her eyes, the back-and-forth movements of her head and those infectious giggles. She loved, deeply. And when you closed your eyes and listened closely, her voice was clear.

Through our profound friendship with Blyth and Charlie, we've come to realize that Havi's voice is still here, still clear, always present. And it will remain with us—forever. ∎

Strong Coffee

JAMIE L.

I tend to give and give, sometimes to my detriment.

Getting a cup of coffee is one way I've found to give back to myself. When I feel let down or disappointed, waiting on someone to show up or call, I know, at least, coffee will be there for me—a friend in the form of espresso and foam. It's reliably helped me through life even if, deep down, I craved something more substantially human.

This comforting routine had always been enough, until something horrible and unthinkable happened. My aunt Cynnie, who I adored with all my heart and for all my life, was unexpectedly diagnosed with cancer.

Now, the act of giving grew larger and more unbearable even as it somehow became more effortless. I gave in love, time, words, and support. I gave in practical ways and emotional ways: car rides, research, updates, and conversations with adults about horrible subjects.

None of this felt like work in a begrudging sense; it was an immediate "rising to meet a need." But it was still exhausting and was corrupting my sense of sanity. I just wanted to grieve, but also didn't want to admit to myself what was happening. I wanted everyone to feel supported, loved, and included. And most of all, I wanted to help my mom, lost in a sea of something I could barely touch: the thought of losing her dearest friend and sister. Oh, and I wanted to save my aunt's life. No big thing.

Six months after her diagnosis, my aunt passed away. I remember the wind in the palm trees when I ran out of the house, the pretty black sky and stars, so cool and impartial and present. I had five minutes to myself before the nurse joined me outside—to talk to me about *her* feelings.

Shortly after, I was swept into a sea of to-dos, a zombie helping to organize two separate memorials, fielding jaunty questions about times, locations, and outfits. *Party planning for the void.* Dizzy with dissonance, I felt as though no one saw how crushed I was. I clung to my coffee ritual, hoping for that familiar sense of support. But now all the coffees in the world seemed about as useful as a Band-Aid on a severed limb.

One day, in this state, I was at home—another creaky morning, trying to wake up. I was sitting on the floor, probably petting my cats, in a lull, in a fog, when my cousin texted and asked for my address.

Before I knew it, a giant, freshly baked, glistening loaf of bread from a hip, nearby French bakery arrived at my door, along with a generous pat of sweet, salted butter and bright, translucent raspberry jam—and a hot, frothy oat milk latte. I received the gift like a swaddled newborn, staring at this display of godly wealth, and cried.

I texted my cousins—all three of them—who had collaborated to arrange this treat. One of them didn't even live in the same state but had nevertheless managed to pick a nearby bakery I barely dared to enter on a regular basis, because it was such a "special" place. Somehow, from miles away, without phone calls or facial expressions, they had seen me. They felt what I was going through and acted on it like little loving spies, conspiring to bring joy to my life, touching my heart when I thought my heart was broken.

I continued to cry and laugh and cry as I cut the bread with a huge knife, using too much butter and jam, and sat on the floor with the hot, sweet oat latte between my hands. The sun came through the window as I ate. I dunked the bread in the latte, ravenous and happy, as beads of oil appeared on the coffee's surface. I was present, alive and in my body; grateful for life, rather than ashamed of it, for the first time in a long time.

The remains of the loaf and butter and jam sat in my fridge for as long as I could get away with it. When the bread was gone, the plastic butter dish remained, for months probably. Every time I saw it, I thought of my cousins—and I thought of Cynnie, who also loved bread and butter and coffee, my cousins, and me. ▪

SPOTLIGHT

When I called to file for short-term disability for breast cancer treatment, the man I talked to ended the call by saying, "You got this." At such a scary time, to have a complete stranger offer that kind of support to me over the phone was so impactful. Kind words mean so much. —*Melody H.*

Airport Angel

SUE R.

The loneliest moment of my life happened while I was surrounded by people. I was traveling to Ann Arbor, Michigan, from my home in Hawaii, catching my final connecting flight at Chicago's bustling O'Hare Airport.

My dad was gravely ill. It had only been two weeks since I'd seen him last, and he'd seemed healthy and vibrant and full of life—we'd had such a good visit! So, when my sister called to tell me he was on his deathbed, I was—well, to say I was shocked is an understatement. We hung up, and I booked the next flight to the mainland.

While waiting to board the final leg of my flight, I mindlessly browsed through magazines, preoccupied with worry. I decided to call the ICU waiting room to get an update from my family, but the person who answered the phone informed me that none of my family members were there. That meant one of two things: Either my father was better and had been moved to a room, or he had passed. I called my sister at her house. The moment she heard my voice, she said, "Oh, Sue …"

> I yearned for a moment of connection—a glimmer of understanding from another human being—but came up empty. I was utterly and completely alone.

I knew in an instant that he was gone. Neither of us could talk through our sobs.

I hung up and shoved my phone back into my purse, blinded by tears and racked with grief. I had to get somewhere private, away from this throng of travelers. I could feel them staring in my direction, but as soon as I looked up, their eyes darted away. I yearned for a moment of connection—a glimmer of understanding from another human being—but came up empty. I was utterly and completely alone.

I rolled my bags into the nearest bathroom, stood at the sink, and cried. My dad was gone, and I didn't get to say goodbye. I didn't make it in time.

Suddenly, I felt a gentle hand on my shoulder. A woman's voice said, "I know something horrible has just happened to you, and I am so sorry."

She didn't tell me her name. She didn't ask me what happened. All she did was stand there with me until my tears slowed, and then quietly waited while I washed my face and pulled myself together. It couldn't have taken more than five minutes, but those five minutes were crucial; I needed to fall apart, but I needed someone with me while it happened. I needed to know that I wasn't alone.

We exited the bathroom, and she vanished. Was she even real? I've asked myself that question many times over the years. When I close my eyes, I can still feel her hand on my shoulder. Sometimes, I wonder if she was an angel.

If I were ever to run into her again, I'd give her a gigantic hug—tell her what a profound difference she made in my life, and what a lasting impression her empathy made. The comfort she provided in that moment was so understated and simple, and yet so powerful. By being present and bearing witness to my pain, she transformed a sterile airport bathroom into a sanctuary.

I was there to board a connecting flight. But she restored my faith in human connection. ∎

Just the
Right Note

AMANDA M.

Before giving birth to our second child in 2018, I'd never truly experienced profound joy and immense suffering at the same time. I thought those feelings would have to take turns coming and going; they sit at opposite ends of a spectrum, after all.

Nope.

When those two emotions converge simultaneously, as they did for me on Mother's Day as I sat in the neonatal ICU, clutching a bag of gifts from strangers and watching my newborn breathe from under a mountain of monitors and tubes, it felt like gratitude.

But let me start at the beginning.

We did everything we were supposed to do to prepare our little family for the big adjustment of a new sibling—I had lists and plans, and backup lists and plans. But none of them accounted for what actually ended up happening. Despite a healthy and uneventful pregnancy and birth, our baby was born fighting for life from the moment he took his first breath.

We were immediately thrown into chaos, transferred to a different hospital two hours away—and in a matter of hours, our family of four was fragmented. Instead of being at home adjusting to our new normal as expected, my mom was at our house caring for our toddler while my husband and I basically lived at the hospital, riding a roller coaster of constant unknowns.

By the time Mother's Day rolled around, we'd been at the hospital for weeks. I was exhausted and emotionally raw; everything felt precarious and fragile, and all I wanted was to go home with my baby. But I was also incredibly thankful for the care he was receiving.

Some days my husband and I had to take it hour by hour,

unsure of whether our boy would live to see another day. Walking through that level of uncertainty changed me; the pain made happy moments all the more profound.

On Mother's Day morning, two women stopped by our room—I think the nurses said they were local moms—with a tote bag full of things like snacks, dry shampoo, lotion, cozy socks, and handwritten notes. They kept their visit short and sweet, saying that they wanted to celebrate me on this special day, even though (or maybe especially because!) I was with my newborn at the hospital. The gifts were incredibly thoughtful, but the notes of encouragement were life preservers I clung to every day until we were finally discharged. Those words gave me something to hold on to when I felt like my world was crumbling, and they were written by people who didn't even know me!

This wasn't the Mother's Day I'd envisioned, but it turned out to be the most beautiful one I've ever had. Nothing prepares you for the experience of a very sick newborn. But in the end, I came away from those harrowing weeks with a new perspective and a fuller understanding of what gratitude truly means. ∎

SPOTLIGHT

A lovely lady at a pain clinic I was going to bought me private restorative yoga lessons during a terrible phase of my chronic illness. I had no money, and she said, "You're too young to be dealing with this." I was in awe … It meant the world to me. —*Sarah R.*

Turning Point

TANYA L.

Inearly died when I was 14, all because of a grilled cheese sandwich. I wish I could say I'd choked on some weirdly unyielding bite—that I'd received the Heimlich maneuver in the nick of time and lived to tell the tale. But the sandwich wasn't the culprit. My mother was.

She was no match for her inner demons, so instead she hit her kids—specifically, me and my older sister. My two younger sisters were never hit, thankfully. On that day, I was the target, physically attacked for missing dinner: a grilled cheese sandwich. Blow after blow, she wailed on my head. When I tried to flee, she came for my throat. I couldn't breathe.

It was OK, I told a friend later. Just another Tuesday evening. It wasn't until I told our school counselor (at my friend's urging) that I confronted reality: This wasn't normal.

I'd hated every Christmas in memory because they so painfully contrasted the Hallmark clichés—everyone lovingly gathered around a tree, giddy over presents, surrounded by scattered wrapping paper. For me, holidays hurt, and images like these rubbed salt in the wound. If my Christmases had a card, they would feature a mother in a snowflake sweater, with the caption: "Tanya's the ugliest of all my daughters."

I internalized that comment, convinced of my hideousness every time I looked in the mirror. I fixated in particular on my skin, the freckles and moles peppering my body. Yes, in an alternate universe, where girls are loved by their mothers, they'd pass as beauty marks. But here, on Grilled Cheese Island, no way. They were blights, a scourge—tiny, bug-like justifications of my mother's rejection.

Four years after I got married and learned I was pregnant, I vowed to become the sort of mother I never had. Never would

I starve my babies of touch and affection, or give them cause to doubt their worth. If, one day, as young adults, a whispering internal voice inquired, "Who could ever love you?" they'd hear their mother like a guiding bell: "I do." I would keep them safe, I thought—never anticipating, five days before my 35th birthday, I'd be diagnosed with cancer.

My whole world was reduced to a single mole on my shoulder. Melanoma. What about my babies, who were only eight and 10? I couldn't breathe. How could I ensure they'd grow up safe and loved? Breathe. How much was I going to miss? First girlfriend, prom and graduation, future spouse, future—I can't breathe—grandchildren?

As worst-case scenarios emerged, I fought them back with an incantation: You're going to be OK. I repeated it over and over, determined to be strong. I had to be strong, for my kids. But who was going to be strong for me?

The day I got the news, I walked into the grocery store, attempting to focus on a shopping list. But the words kept dropping off, rearranging themselves into a jumbled mess. We needed milk. I have cancer. Canned peaches, spaghetti sauce. I have cancer. People strolled past with their rattling carts, perusing shelves, reading ingredients, like today was just a normal day, which—unbelievably—it was. I was just one person of thousands who passed through here every day. What am I going to do? We need milk. What will happen if I—

"You look beautiful in your dress."

The voice—steady and kind—definitely didn't belong to me. I looked up, my storm of anxiety dissipating long enough to reveal a smiling lady with her elderly mom. She'd given me a compliment, I realized. So, naturally, I replied.

"I just found out I have cancer."

As the words left my mouth, my eyes welled up—whatever strength I'd attempted to cobble together crumbling instantly. She was a perfect stranger—hardly an "appropriate" person from whom to seek comfort. I waited for the ensuing awkwardness—averted eyes, a murmured "I'm sorry"—before she fled.

Instead, she wrapped her arms around me. It didn't feel like a stranger's hug, rigid with formality. Instead, it was warm, enveloping, and safe—the embrace of a mother. I fell apart in her arms, and she let me, absorbing my tears, holding my pain. "It isn't an accident that we met today," she said. "I feel it deep in my bones—we were meant to meet. And you know what I think?"

I waited, terrified, for my verdict. Surely, kindness came with a price. I waited for the inevitable slap—the moment she'd tell me, "Stop being a baby, look reality in the face, deal with it."

I was going to die.

"You're going to be OK."

She spoke quietly, face half-buried in my hair, holding me together, waiting for her words to soak like balm into my skin. The incantation I'd repeated for myself, which had, despite my own efforts, sounded so hollow, now washed over me like an inner knowing. I'm going to be OK.

As of August 2022, I'm clear of cancer. I can't thank that woman enough for being the mother I'd always needed—for holding the weight of my world for just a little while. ▪

Debt of Gratitude

DANIELLE L.

I love the NHS—formally known as the United Kingdom's National Health Service—universal health care provided free at point of entry. How great is that? Even as a member of staff—fielding the effects of Brexit and COVID, stretched thin in money, energy, support—I still love the NHS. There's just something so British about it: everyone exhausted, yet sucking it up for the greater good, putting on a brave face and the kettle for a cuppa—because that's all you can do, isn't it? Keep calm and carry on.

In fact, as I waved goodbye to my colleague at the end of our nine-and-a-half-hour shift and started up my car, the sole thing on my mind was a nice hot cup of tea. The bubbling of boiling water. The clink of the spoon. The horrifyingly loud crunching thump of my car reversing into another object.

Wait, what?

No, no, no—I'd backed into another car!

I rushed out to assess the damage, heart in my throat. I clamped a hand over my mouth. There, on the passenger door of a gray Toyota: a dent the size of a footballer's head. What have I done? The door would definitely need fixing—but, would it need replacing? How much was that? I didn't know. Oh God, and add to that a paint job, labor … visions of pending poverty danced in my head.

My car had suffered minimal damage, but that was mine; I could deal with it by not fixing it. To pay for this fiasco, though, I'd have no choice but to put a claim on my insurance—and at the worst possible time, when bills were skyrocketing (the government anticipated a price increase of up to 80 percent on energy). I'd lose my no-claims discount, and my monthly payments would go up by at least 50 percent.

I worked part-time as a receptionist; picking up an extra shift wasn't an option. Where would I find the extra money every month? And what if the car's owner towed his chariot to one of those fancy, extortionist garages from hell? I felt so helpless, subject to the vagaries of fate—my whole life irrevocably dented.

I left a note on the damaged car's windshield, writing it with all the enthusiasm as my last will and testament.

A day went by, then two. A whole week passed before the car's owner, David, finally got in touch. The dread had been building and building, so I was glad to finally talk to him and apologize personally. He said he'd get a quote on the damage and get back to me. I swallowed. The process had begun. Though David was lovely and kind, I still had to wait and see how much it was going to be.

I was at work when David finally got back to me: He wanted nothing.

I blinked at the message and read it again. "Consider it a token of appreciation for all the hard work NHS workers have put in to keep the NHS running." I couldn't believe it. Nobody could. To forgive a debt like that during a time when money was tight for everyone—it was incredible. Though it was completely within his right to demand payment, he chose instead to make an unparalleled act of generosity—an act with effects that continue to ripple outward through my life.

> I felt so helpless, subject to the vagaries of fate— my whole life irrevocably dented.

To this day, I can't believe it. He owed me nothing. I owe him everything. ∎

One Last Wave

DANIEL F.

My dad passed away March 12, 2019—one year before the pandemic hit the States full force. The timing was weird. After a year of deeply personal grief, during which I felt somewhat removed from society, the world changed. Isolation, fear, the fragility of life—suddenly, these topics went from being taboo to all anyone could talk about.

Still, three years later, people have long stopped calling to talk about my dad—to check in, ask how I'm doing. Though his death continues to feel very new to me, it's ancient history to them—as it should be. That's how it goes. My mother and I talk often and have spent every anniversary of his death together in Vermont, honoring him. But still—it's not the same. The pandemic may have transformed grief into a national conversation, but I wanted a one-on-one. And the person with whom I wanted to talk most was, of course, my dad.

The thing is, even when he was alive, my dad wasn't much of a talker. He was always a great sounding board, but when it came to verbalizing—not really his thing. In terms of sharing emotions, same deal. He *embodied* love—demonstrated it daily with his actions, his steady presence. Instead of putting things into words, we bonded through adventures: tackling mountains, traversing deserts, plumbing the depths of the deep blue sea.

My dad was a lot like the ocean, actually: elemental, powerful, always there. I think that's why I feel so connected to him when I surf—why one day I spontaneously wrote his name on the nose of my surfboard—so we could commune with the ocean together. Out on the waves, I felt his presence so strongly: a great force churning under my board, catapulting me forward through life. But, back on dry land, I was alone again, putting one foot in front of the other.

No more cries of wheeling gulls. No more propulsive currents and crashing water. Just stillness. Interminable quiet.

In January 2022, I created the One Last Wave Project, an online venture dedicated to helping bereaved folks process their grief. It was inspired by the spontaneous act of inscribing my father's name on my board. It meant so much to me to see it there—dipping in and out of the waves, embarking on one last adventure—that I posted a video to TikTok inviting people to add the names of anyone they'd lost. I'm not sure I expected anyone to respond.

Now, grieving families contact me every day, sharing the names of their deceased loved ones so I can take them out on the water. I've received pages upon pages about the lives they had, the things they accomplished, the dreams they had, and their impact on the world. One by one, I add their names to my board—just me, my dad, and thousands of cherished strangers.

On March 12, 2022, I received my first email from a woman named Marlene. She'd just received a terminal cancer diagnosis, and, in response, jumped online, determined to take fate into her own hands.

As we started emailing back and forth, uncanny similarities to my father began to reveal themselves. For instance, they'd both been diagnosed with pancreatic cancer. Or, years ago, she'd worked as a nurse—in the same hospital where he'd received palliative care. Even their names—Marlene, Karl—echoed one another: a kind of assonance, if not a rhyme.

But there was something else,

too—an ineffable quality they shared. Like my dad, Marlene had a powerful sense of herself in the world. She was strong. A dreamer. A connecting force. My dad did everything in his power to ensure he'd die in a place he loved—looking out over the cow pasture of his farm in Vermont—just as Marlene found a way to be with the ocean. Fittingly, her name means "star of the sea," and that's what she was—a surfer, a sea maiden. In one email, she described herself as "a palm tree, not a pine tree."

Which brings me to my next point. For all the ways she resembled my dad, there was one way they couldn't be more different. Marlene *loved* language. Words were her jam.

Now, I'm not the kind of person who looks for "signs" or hidden meanings—but that said, I don't think human perception has an absolute lock on reality. There's no way our five puny senses have the capacity to process life in all its infinite, confounding complexity.

Which is all to say that in some strange way, I felt Marlene and my dad shared a spiritual bond. Like I said, words weren't his thing, so it was remarkable to meet someone so similar to him, and yet so opposite on that particular front. I like to think he sent Marlene as a sort of emissary—a person through whom he could finally communicate with words. After all, he was dead. I wasn't. And Marlene—she was someplace in between, connecting us both.

It didn't occur to me until months later, but that first email she sent arrived on the third anniversary of my dad's death. Maybe it's a coincidence; maybe it's a sign. Either way, I'm eternally grateful. Thanks to this vibrant, singular woman, who was only in my life for a few months, I finally got a taste of what it might be like to connect to my father through words. Brave, life-affirming, and fun, she showed me through her emails how conversation—like climbing mountains, or diving under waves—can be an adventure, too. ∎

SPOTLIGHT

I was going through a breakup after a long relationship and wasn't eating. A co-worker who barely knew me started packing lunches for two, so that I would eat with her. —*Valerie C.*

CHAPTER SIX

Away From Home

It's a beautiful world

Buen Viaje

MICHELE L.

I fell in love with ancient Maya culture through a National Geographic book titled *The Mysterious Maya*. In high school, an exchange program in Mexico convinced me I'd live there one day—and after college, I made good on that prediction. But, after spending a few years as a social worker, I became frustrated with the overly complex systems of aid: the red tape that kept people from seeking and receiving help.

Fortunately, a co-worker introduced me to a volunteer organization in the Yucatán that worked to provide direct support to families in the capital city of Mérida and its surrounding villages. I knew it was the kind of job where I could directly impact people's lives—no red tape and no convoluted structures.

I loved living in Mérida. People there are friendly and self-deprecating, with strong work ethics. They are also artistically inclined (I often wound up at public poem and song nights downtown). Yucatecans are also known for their generosity, which often involves pleasing others over themselves. I learned this firsthand one afternoon.

Although my official volunteer job had ended, I still occasionally delivered groceries and school supplies to families in need. I'd often make several visits in a day, usually when children weren't in school, sometimes bringing gifts as well. Food, drawings, small crafts, and more were frequently given to me to pass on to U.S.-based sponsor families. When I made these trips, I carried all my important documents in my bag, as I was transitioning from one visa to another. I also carried my only two credit cards and a sizable amount of cash.

After finishing my deliveries one day, I returned my organization's car and was walking home when I realized I didn't have my bag. I had no copies of the documents inside. I briefly panicked, but assumed I had left everything in the car, and planned to call the organization when I got home.

That's when I saw Don Eladio. He looked to be in his late 70s, and was sitting on the sidewalk with his back against the wall surrounding my house. He saw me approaching, then stood up and smiled, saying, "Good afternoon! You're the gringa I was looking for!" He proudly unfurled my now dirty, rolled-up bag from inside his.

I unrolled the bag to discover all my documents, credit cards, and cash still tucked into a side pocket. I couldn't believe my carelessness. But dwarfing this was a rush of gratitude toward this elderly stranger standing outside my house. I asked his name, and he introduced himself before telling his story.

Don Eladio lived in a remote Maya village and had made his usual two-hour trip (via multiple buses and vans) into Mérida, where he offered up yard work door-to-door. It was impossible to tell exactly where he'd found my bag, because, like many others from the surrounding villages, he couldn't read and had to rely on landmarks to navigate. I had made many stops across multiple neighborhoods that day; he was already on his way home when he found my bag. And though he didn't know what all my documents inside were, he told me they "looked very important."

It would be easy to characterize someone like Don Eladio as "dignified" or "humble," imposing noble, poetic, or even saintly traits onto him. But this would strip him of his humanity, remaking him into something more comfortable to comprehend and further away from myself.

Because he couldn't read the address on my ID, Don Eladio had to ask several people for help. Once my neighborhood was located, he took a bus downtown to the central hub and began asking more strangers which bus he should take to get to me. With his only remaining money for the day, he bought a ticket in my direction and asked the bus driver where to get off. He then began knocking on doors until he was finally pointed to my home, where he waited a few hours for my return.

After all this, he refused to take a reward from me (all the more staggering, considering the cash in my bag was more than he made in two weeks). He accepted enough money for a bus ride home and was on his way, as he knew his wife would be worried about him returning late.

It would be easy to characterize someone like Don Eladio as "dignified" or "humble," imposing noble, poetic, or even saintly traits onto him. But this would strip him of his humanity, remaking him into something more comfortable to comprehend and further away from myself. Of course, that doesn't mean I didn't cry my eyes out as soon as he left, as the full weight of his gesture sank in.

This was a man who risked judgment and ridicule from urbanite strangers across the city in his journey to find me. He painted himself a target by carrying my bag and showing people what was inside as he walked through a dangerous neighborhood. Twenty-five years later, I still get emotional thinking about it.

I had come to the Yucatán because of a childhood dream; getting to help people while I lived there and explored the culture was a bonus. Maybe it's ironic that the help I received remains one of my biggest takeaways from living there. But throughout my travels, I've noticed over and over that those with the fewest resources are often the ones most likely to help others—no matter the risks. There's no clean and tidy lesson to pull from that, but it warrants saying regardless. ▪

SPOTLIGHT

When I was a little kid, I was on vacation walking the beach with my family. It was a cold and windy Oregon coast day, and I was bored, so I started using my foot to dig my name into the sand to see it get filled with the next tide. This older gentleman must have thought I was searching for pretty souvenirs to take home. So, he walks over and hands me a huge handful of the most beautiful, smooth agates. They were still warm from his hands, and had probably taken at least all day to gather along the beach. It was so sweet. —*Kait F.*

A Welcome Distraction

ANNIE F.

When I was in my mid-20s, I traveled to Ireland to work as an intern at a retreat center. I love to travel, and it was the perfect time in my life for an adventure. My co-workers and I planned to backpack across the country after our internship ended, and I wasn't really sure when I'd return to the United States.

Several months later, my plans came to an abrupt halt, thanks to an evil stomach virus that descended upon us. Everyone else got better—I did not—and none of the doctors could figure it out. After six weeks of not being able to stomach solid food, I lost 20 pounds. I was gravely ill, and my mother, who is a registered nurse, begged me to come home.

Frail, queasy, and without options, I made my way to Dublin Airport. Because I was taking in so little food and water, I was constantly on the verge of passing out. I knew if I fainted in the airport, someone would call an ambulance and I'd end up at the ER (a place I'd grown all too familiar with by this point). I also knew the doctors there wouldn't be able to help. So my task was to accomplish the seemingly impossible: Stay conscious long enough to make it home.

I'm a very independent person, and being vulnerable terrified me. Moving slowly, I checked my luggage, hitched up the jeans falling off my body, pulled my long dark hair into a ponytail, and made up my mind: I was going to make it.

By the time I landed in Chicago, I hadn't slept in nearly 24 hours and was *not* doing well. I shuffled to the gate for the final connecting flight from Chicago to St. Louis, only to learn we had a one- to two-hour delay. At this point, even a 10-minute delay felt like a lifetime, and I truly began to question whether or not I was going to die. I considered what would happen if I was brought to a hospital in Chicago, calculating how long it would take for my mom to reach me by car.

I dropped my backpack on the floor and positioned my body against it, focusing on staying awake without falling apart. I'd been taking care of myself for weeks, and I was absolutely exhausted. I just wanted my mom.

But then an amazing thing happened. A toddler wandered over, interested in talking to me. Her eyes were bright, and when I smiled at her, her face lit up. Her mother called out—Anaïs!—and apologized for the disturbance. I shook my head emphatically.

"This is a welcome distraction, believe me."

In the next few hours, Anaïs and I became best friends. We looked at the airplanes outside as she played with the blinds on the big windows. I sat up a little straighter, pretending not to be on death's doorstep. Her mother was a single parent returning from Europe, and she ended up telling me her story and struggles. It

brought me out of my suffering and distracted me so much that I felt more like a normal human again. A connection—exactly what I needed to get me through.

Time flew by, and before long it was time to board my flight. I bid Anaïs and her mother goodbye, dragged myself into yet another airplane, and flew home to my mom. Finally.

I found out later that I'd had what is known as post-viral gastroparesis, which is quite serious. The virus permanently damaged the nerves that control the muscles in my stomach. Everything changed after that experience, from my lifestyle and diet to how I view the world.

But persevering through tremendous difficulty allowed me to experience extraordinary grace. I am forever grateful to the mother and daughter who appeared at just the right time, giving me a distraction in the exact moment I needed it. Without having faced something so hard, I'd never have experienced beauty so bright. ∎

New York State of Kind

SARAH B.

If you grow up in Australia, it's a rite of passage to travel after high school. Not one to break with tradition, I embarked on a long trip through Europe in 1992, shortly after turning 19, that would eventually bring me to New York. I'd had the time of my life in Europe—or, to put it another way, I'd blown through most of my budget. By the time I made it to the United States, I'd achieved full vagabond status. ("Give me your tired, your poor"—indeed.)

But I was a fearless teenager, so my lack of funds didn't worry me. That is, until the pilot announced we would soon be landing in Newark, New Jersey. "I got on the wrong plane!" I exclaimed to the flight attendant. "We're just one bridge away, dear," she said. A bus would take me from Newark to Port Authority in Manhattan, she explained, and it would take only 30 minutes. Phew!

I got off the bus in Manhattan very early on a cold Sunday morning. I sported a giant purple puffer, stuffed with down as light as my suitcase was heavy. I heave-hoed my luggage through the bustling station in search of an information desk, where I hoped someone would point me in the direction of a youth hostel.

As I searched, a man approached me and asked if I'd like some help carrying my suitcase. I told him I appreciated the offer but could handle it on my own. He didn't like that answer, and became increasingly angry each time I refused. I suppose my argumentative Aussie accent garnered attention, because suddenly a petite young woman in business attire stormed our way, using her hard-boiled New York know-how to call off the man. As he skulked away, defeated, she extended a jaunty hand.

"I'm Audrey," she said. "Are you OK?"

After thanking her, I told her I was from Australia—here for just a few days—and currently in search of a youth hostel. She warned me off youth hostels in the area—too dangerous—but added she'd happily help me find another place to stay.

Audrey had been an exchange student in Australia a few years prior, so naturally we started to discuss our favorite Aussie spots. When I asked why she was dressed so professionally on a Sunday morning, she laughed, explaining that she was an accountant, returning home from a late night out with her co-worker friends. Our conversation flowed so easily that I already felt like we were old friends.

> Things could have gone so wrong on that trip, but they didn't. I owe that completely to Audrey, a complete stranger who looked out for me.

Still, it surprised me when she said I could stay at her apartment. I knew it was sort of weird, but the combination of her being nice and me being broke made it impossible to say no. So I went with it. I followed her onto another bus, and together we rode through Manhattan to Hoboken. We made a funny pair—Audrey in her tailored work clothes, me in my enormous purple puffer (I looked a little like Princess Di tackling the slopes—the broke-on-a-bus version.)

Audrey shared a two-bedroom in a red brick building with her roommate and fellow accountant, Julie, who welcomed me just as warmly as Audrey had. We ate breakfast together and planned my sightseeing for the next few days. Audrey even gave me her Australian host family's number to give to my parents, so they wouldn't be worried. My parents called the family, who reassured them Audrey, their beloved (if temporary) American daughter, wasn't going to kidnap me.

I stayed with Audrey for about a week, sightseeing all day and hanging out with her at night. We cooked together, took trips to the deli next door, and spent time on her roof, which had a perfect view of the Manhattan skyline.

I was a teenager when Audrey and I met, and as a result was fairly naive. Before our paths crossed, I don't think I believed in "kindness to strangers"—at least, not to that extent. Things could have gone so wrong on that trip, but they didn't. I owe that completely to Audrey, a complete stranger who looked out for me. In addition to providing sanctuary and friendship, she reshaped my view of humanity—and myself—with her kindness. We stayed in touch briefly as pen pals by mail after I went home, but being pre-internet days, we eventually lost touch.

Since that trip, if I ever face something scary, I just think: I turned up to New York City with nothing and I lived to tell the tale. I fall on my feet and things work out, even when I'm not sure they will.

I can't thank Audrey enough for allowing me to see the world through that lens. ▪

SPOTLIGHT

Edinburgh. I was freezing, it was raining hard, and I was walking fast toward my B&B that was still a good 20 blocks away. No cash on me. A couple was outside bringing something inside their house. They saw me, invited me into their home, and gave me hot tea and cookies. They let me stay until it stopped raining and told me the most entertaining stories about their lives. I never felt such warmth and gratitude. —*Alejandra B.*

Lend a Hand

REBECCA R.

In my early 20s, I joined my colleagues on a work trip. Midway through our flight, we were met with what's colloquially known as turbulence (though I prefer the term "hell"). The plane shook and dipped aggressively. Carry-on luggage banged loudly overhead.

I exhaled, telling myself it would be over soon—but it wasn't. As the turbulence continued, tears welled up. The plane is going to crash, I thought. I'll never see the people I love again. I'm going to die.

I usually flew with friends, a source of comfort when turbulence struck. But this time, I felt alone. As I gripped the armrests in panic, I noticed a man and woman across the aisle staring. Great, I thought. They think I'm crazy.

I was in the aisle seat, and the man was in the aisle seat next to mine. Suddenly, he stretched out his arm and opened his palm. I grabbed it immediately, holding on for dear life. Twenty minutes into this death grip, he never once wavered. Tears continued to stream down my face. He continued to be there.

When the quaking finally subsided, I thanked the man and his wife profusely. They were so gracious, insisting it was no big deal. While an outstretched hand may have not meant much to them, it meant the world to me. ∎

A Knight in Shining Armor

KAELEEN K.

A lot of people say their lives changed while studying abroad. But mine changed on my way to study abroad, thanks to a spunky stunt double.

I was 18 years old and had just flown in from my hometown in Oregon to San Francisco, where I planned to catch a connecting flight to London. Anxious by nature, I found that traveling compounded my stress level by a thousand. (For those fortunate enough not to know, that's code for I cried a lot.)

I landed safely in San Francisco, but an issue on the tarmac delayed deplaning. After waiting, oh, two million years to exit the aircraft, I frantically raced to the gate to make my next flight. I was too late. The plane had (heartlessly) taken off without me—and the next one wasn't due until the following day. Adding to an already crappy situation, the gate agent informed me all nearby hotels were booked, and that the airport closes for two hours in the middle of the night—meaning I couldn't camp out there, either.

As I stood there with my puffy eyes and baggy clothes (it was 2005), all alone with nowhere to go, all I could think was that I obviously cannot manage without my mom and need to send myself home. Over and over, on a loop, in keeping with the grand tradition of anxiety.

Maybe I'd still be standing in that spot today, frozen with fear, paralyzed with puffiness, if an unconventional superwoman hadn't

> Before I met Emma, I believed my mother was the only person capable of caring for me unconditionally. But I was wrong.

intervened. I saw her approach from the corner of my eye: unusually short, spiky blond bob, tight black clothes, a choker. She'd been nearby while I was speaking with the agent, so she knew what was going on.

"This is silly," she announced. "Just come home with me. My nephew"—she points to a boy my age—"is visiting from London, and missed his flight, too. Stay with us, and then we'll all come back here tomorrow."

Her name was Emma, and she was fantastic, distracting me from my woes with a series of self-deprecating jokes. She didn't look like my mother; my mom dressed and spoke much more conservatively than Emma. But her presence felt maternal to me.

The gate agent let me use her phone to call my mom, and Emma spoke with her as well; she was so kind and comforting. And so, listening to my gut (and my mother), I agreed to go home with her and her British nephew.

Her house—tiny, yellow, surrounded by flowers—looked exactly like the kind of house a person like Emma would have. She was a Hollywood stunt double, so the place was full of movie props: trinkets, posters, and—most notably—a full-size suit of armor. She insisted on comfort food for dinner, so we ate fried chicken in the living room and passed the time cracking jokes. Eventually, it was time for bed, and she gave me the guest bedroom. I fell asleep with Emma's two hairless cats curled up at my feet, cozy and content.

We woke at sunrise, picked up doughnuts, and arrived at the airport three hours early to avoid further problems. Emma cajoled the gate agent into seating me and her nephew next to each other. We hugged her goodbye and boarded the flight.

Before I met Emma, I believed my mother was the only person capable of caring for me unconditionally. But I was wrong. A perfect stranger, motivated by nothing more than the goodness of her heart, saved me from a fearful night alone. She offered me not only a place to sleep, but also a new perspective: a sense of agency in a chaotic world.

Now, when I'm anxious, I access the memory of that night, returning to Emma's little yellow house to bask in her warmth and laughter. I'm OK, I realize. At times, I wonder if that suit of armor in her living room isn't so much a prop as a sign of who she was— not a damsel in distress, but a knight. A protector. ▪

Opportunity Knocks

RACHEL R.

I'd been searching for an apartment in Los Angeles for months. Every place I looked at was mostly fine, but with a dash of horror. A creeping death stain on a bedroom ceiling. Wall-to-wall carpeting in a desiccated shade of brown. A weirdly truncated peacock green bathtub—built specifically, it seemed, for sobbing in the fetal position.

Still, I needed a place. So I resolved to settle, to make peace with horror. Or at least make peace with some run-of-the-mill inconveniences—no parking, for instance. No laundry. Perfect doesn't exist, I reminded myself. Especially at my budget.

But then, I found it. The perfect apartment.

A small building owned by a sweet older couple on a quiet, tree-lined street. Walking distance to restaurants and shops. Private laundry room, easy parking. Tons of sunlight, hardwood floors. *Reasonable rent.* How did this happen? I felt like I'd been scrolling through dating apps for years, fielding interminable messages from the Mayors of Red Flag City, and—somehow—woke up happily married to "Hey Girl" Ryan Gosling. Surely, there's a catch, I thought (nevertheless leaping to sign the lease). Surely, the other shoe will drop.

Well, the other shoe didn't drop. My neighbor's bass did.

I arrived at my new front door, clothing-stuffed trash bags in tow, to a fanfare of decidedly bad vibrations. *Bzzzzz-BZZ!-BZZ!-bzzzzzzzzzzz.* My heart sank. Inside my apartment, the sound was even worse, like a swarm of bees communicating exclusively in Morse code, broken intermittently by Jurassic booms. It's fine, I told myself. It's Saturday.

But the same thing happened Monday. And Tuesday. And Wednesday and—OK, so this bass wasn't an aberration. It was permanent. A thing I'd have to live with. Somehow.

I should mention: I'm pretty conflict-avoidant. I *really* didn't want to confront my neighbor, not this soon, not right out of the gate.

I played it out in my mind: Knocking timidly on her door. The flash of annoyance when she saw me—New Neighbor, anti-bassist killjoy—commandeering her porch. With a tight smile, she'd acquiesce to my request and turn down the music, but not enough, never enough; I'd always hear it thumping through the wall, slowly, inexorably driving me mad. Eventually, I'd knock again. This time, she'd get defensive. Or maybe not open the door at all. Maybe crank up the bass in a show of resistance, forcing me to, what? Call the police? Maybe. If it got bad enough. A video of me would soon go viral, cementing my place in the *Karen Calls Police* firmament. A star would be born. I'd move out. Change my name. Adopt a lizard.

OK, so, yes—a stretch. The more mature part of me—the part I'd spent years cultivating in therapy—knew this scenario wasn't likely. But, somehow, I couldn't get my very grown-up brain to communicate to my heart, which was pounding, wildly, giving that bass a run for its money.

I'm sure moving had something to do with it. I felt like a hermit crab between shells, unprotected, vulnerable, forced to adapt to a new environment that, for all I knew, could be hostile. On top of all that, it was Valentine's Day, so I felt extra on my own.

The last guy I'd loved, a clarinetist—let's call him Biff—couldn't handle conflict, either. We'd return to his place after a date, and, more often than not, he'd grumble about his "dumb" neighbors, who'd once again blocked his door with their "stupid" baby stroller.

> I should mention: I'm pretty conflict-avoidant. I *really* didn't want to confront my neighbor, not this soon, not right out of the gate.

Eventually, I asked if he'd ever said anything to them. "There's no point," he groused. Instead of risking conflict, I realized, he chose to roll over. To just—*stew*. (When he broke up with me over the phone, I guess I shouldn't have been surprised.)

So, it felt important, like a sort of St. Valentine's Day test, to choose courage over cowardice, communication over resentment. Don't be like Biff, I thought, willing myself to knock on my neighbor's door. From within the apartment, laughter mingled with music. Ugh, I thought to myself. You're such a party pooper.

The door swung open. My neighbor gasped. "Oh no! It's the music, right? Is it too loud?"

"Oh, it's just the bass," I assured her. "The music isn't—"

"I was *just* saying, I hope the bass isn't too loud!" She shook her head, her face a wellspring of humor and understanding. "I'm still figuring out these new speakers." Scrolling through her phone, she pulled up the app. "Oh my god." She threw back her head and peeled with laughter, calling back to her husband and daughter. "The bass is at *nine!* It's, like, at the *highest* setting!" Back to me: *"I'm so sorry."*

As if her response weren't rewarding enough, to my surprise, she invited me inside. Within minutes, we were sitting around the table, digging into slices of chocolate cake, and laughing like old friends. I couldn't believe it. She could not have been more opposite to the nightmare scenario I'd painted for myself. Briefly, I imagined a world in which I hadn't knocked, in which I'd submitted to my inner Biff, stoking quiet animus against my neighbor—who was, it turned out, the Nicest Woman in the World.

The amount of gratitude I felt toward her—not only for being so kind, but for unknowingly rewarding me, the anxious hermit crab next door, for doing something a *little* out of her comfort zone—is hard to quantify. ■

SPOTLIGHT

A stranger blocked traffic with his motorcycle by turning it sideways so that I could cross the street with my baby in a stroller. It was on an island in Greece where there aren't any traffic lights, and nobody was letting us pass. It was a small gesture, but it meant the world to me. —*Maria K.*

Search and
Rescue

BROOKE S.

Running through a dense forest in sandals with a block heel is something I do not recommend.

Had I known that morning what I'd be doing after work, I would have chosen any other pair of shoes. I sobbed as I scaled fallen tree trunks and crashed through thick underbrush, blinded by tears.

Only moments before, everything was fine. It's funny how one decision, like whether or not to put your dog on a lead for a second, can derail your life—but I guess I should start at the beginning.

I can't remember a time in my childhood, growing up in the U.K. and in Spain, when we didn't have at least one dog. I always loved the idea of having one myself, but being a single woman with a full-time office job and a social life made that challenging.

In 2020, the start-up tech company where I work decided to go permanently remote. I loved my job, and by working from home, I finally felt I was in a position to have a dog. The moment I saw a photo of four-week-old Milo, I knew he was the one for me. He's an interesting mix of Chihuahua and something else, with a huge personality despite his tiny size.

Milo changed my life for the better, as dogs always do. While I worked remotely, we spent time in some of my favorite places in Spain. But something about Ibiza kept drawing me back. It has a reputation for being a party island, but there's a whole other side that is both serene and beautiful. Many free-spirited young professionals live there, so I decided to set up shop at an Airbnb for several months.

I found a dog-friendly co-working space that offered Wi-Fi in a beautiful, chilled-out setting. Milo napped or played while I worked.

One Friday evening, 6 p.m. rolled around and found me ready to close out my workweek and hit the bar in the co-working space. But first, I walked Milo to a grassy area where he could do his business. Milo was excited, too, but not because it was Friday; he'd found a chunk of Styrofoam on the ground. As he started to play with it, I tried to grab it from him. But being a playful puppy, he thought it was a game. He began bouncing around, looking back as if to say, "Come get me, Mum!" I realized too late that not only did he not have his lead on, but that he was also getting dangerously close to a busy road.

The next few moments felt like a slow-motion nightmare. As I waved my arms and called his name, Milo dashed out into the road. A car flew right over his tiny body without stopping; miraculously, his small size kept him from being crushed. He tumbled out onto the other side, now missing his collar, and ran into the forest across the road. Without thinking, I ran after him like a lunatic, crashing into the dense woods, platform sandals and all.

It quickly became clear that I wasn't going to find him without my running shoes and some help. I hurried back to my car to swap footwear and find my phone. Tears streaming down my face, I was in a complete panic as people approached me to ask what was wrong. Before I knew it, all sorts of kind people were offering to help find Milo.

Those who were helping with the search called their friends and asked them to look, too; a post went out on social media. Together, we formed a legit search party to scour the woods until midnight.

Total strangers had shown up, prepared with flashlights, food, and battery packs to keep our phones working.

Two different members of the search party had spotted Milo from far away. Just knowing he was still out there filled me with hope, but also dread; just thinking about him alone out there broke my heart.

Something that really touched me, that I didn't find out about until later, was that some of the locals who saw the posts on social media came out to drive slowly on the busy road surrounding the forest so that traffic would be forced to slow down, just in case Milo attempted to go back into the road. People on this island really look after each other.

My best friend Katie was one of the first to arrive with provisions, along with her dog, Disco. They stayed the whole night with me, sleeping on the forest floor and praying that if we were there, Milo might try to find us.

When the sun finally rose, I took stock of the situation. We were covered in cuts and bruises. People began showing up with coffee and pastries, and Katie decided she needed her first coffee in seven

years. The search started again. All told, it was 20 hours before I finally received the call that Milo had been found.

Somehow, he'd wandered into someone's garden and was seen guzzling water from a bowl. The couple living there didn't think much of it, as they live in a popular dog-walking area. But moments later, when they saw Milo's photo on social media, they brought him inside and called. When I saw him, I fell to the floor and sobbed. Milo was weak, but remarkably intact.

I couldn't believe he had survived the ordeal. But even more, I couldn't believe how many kind and selfless people spent so many hours with no other motivation than helping a dog get home. For weeks after, people would stop us on the street because they recognized Milo and were happy to see him safe and healthy.

See? Humans aren't so bad after all. ∎

Give-and-Take

LAUREN H.

When I was 21, I went Interrailing for the first time. The experience is a bit of a rite of passage for young adults without steady incomes in the U.K.: Purchase a ticket that works on train lines across Europe, then milk it for all it's worth for 30 days.

Key tip for the savvy traveler: Sleep on the overnight train instead of spending money on nightly lodging.

My partner and I took our first big trip together across Europe after spending a few days in Paris. Aside from splurging on two nights at an Airbnb, I booked our lodging at cheap hostels and two-star hotels; when these weren't available, I planned for us to sleep on the overnight train. Along for the ride: smartphones and an iPad boasting every map app imaginable, multiple pre-bookmarked local guides, and a fancy digital camera primed to capture every moment. Thanks in no small part to this preparation, the first half of our trip was magical, all of it recorded on my beloved camera.

Twice on our journey, my partner and I were lucky enough to board trains with beds, but the overnight train to Budapest was not among them. Waking up after a few hours of bad sleep in my seat, I noticed one of our bags was missing—the one with all our electronics. I'd never had anything stolen before, let alone items key to survival. So, naturally, my first impulse was to fully disassociate.

In Austria, we spent hours in the police department—time wasted, ultimately. My partner and I did what any vigilantes for justice would do: aimlessly wandered the streets with a bottle of wine. Our drunken, paranoid daze continued through the Czech

> I'd never had anything stolen before, let alone items key to survival. So, naturally, my first impulse was to fully disassociate.

Republic and into Brussels, where we'd booked our Airbnb.

We wandered the train station, looking for anything that could help us—local maps, guides, a single clue—but with little success. The burden of the past few days, made literal by the weight of my gigantic backpack, was finally too much to bear. Just as I'd resolved to give up, a man approached with a question.

"Are you lost?"

He asked again in another language when we were too dumb-struck to answer. "Yes," I replied finally, explaining our sad situation as succinctly as possible. I showed him the Airbnb address. With a brisk nod, he said he knew just what to do and swiftly led the way.

We followed with some hesitation—after all, not all people were to be trusted—as he showed us where to buy tram tickets. Then, he actually followed us on board, making sure we headed in the right direction, and calmly told us exactly how to get to the address from our tram stop. We were able to find the Airbnb easily.

Expecting the host to be there, I broke down in tears when no one answered the doorbell. The next-door neighbor noticed and, much like the man at the station, helped us before we had to ask, calling our host. Apparently, he'd messaged us the day before with instructions—instructions we naturally never received.

Because we'd missed the window for his assistant, who nor-mally let guests in, our host assured us he'd arrive himself within a half hour. Meanwhile, his neighbor offered to take us in while we waited. I was overwhelmed, both by all the unexpected generosity and the ease with which it was expressed. I had emotional whip-lash—a happy version of it, but nonetheless, disorienting.

It now seems rather obvious, but by the end of the trip, I was sur-prised to discover I remembered the people I met much more than the places I visited—especially the people in Brussels. The casual rescue from three strangers will stay with me forever. It's strange that it took someone pinching our bag to create the space for such won-derful memories. I guess some people take—but most of us give. ∎

SPOTLIGHT

I was 10 years old, alone on a train from Morioka, Japan, to Tokyo. I had been visiting a friend and her mom out in the country and was returning back to the city to meet my dad, who was there on business.

Homesick, I must have looked uneasy, as an old Japanese man who spoke no English looked across the aisle and gave me a thumbs-up to make sure I was OK. I tentatively gave him one back, and eventually dozed off. When I woke up in Tokyo, I realized that the old man had put his suit jacket on me as a blanket. He smiled when I thanked him as he collected his coat.

I'll likely never see him again, but I'll always feel protected by that man, a kind soul and guardian in a foreign place. —*Dee N.*

Warmhearted

IRIS S.

When I graduated high school at the tender age of 17, I had one thing in mind: getting off the island of Puerto Rico. I'd always planned to move to the contiguous United States; it sounded so exciting, romantic, and adventurous. Wasting no time landing a full-time job that would get me there, I signed a contract without closely reading it first, resulting in a job located in Pennsylvania.

Pennsylvania?!

When I agreed to take a job on the mainland, I imagined New York City or Los Angeles!

Nope.

Provided a one-way ticket and a start date, I was told to pack my bags. Naturally, I packed nearly my whole wardrobe, consisting entirely of clothing for Puerto Rico's steamy climate. It didn't occur to me, growing up with balmy Octobers, that Pennsylvania at that time of year would be cold.

On departure day, I practically skipped into the San Juan airport, full of excitement and anticipation. I absolutely adore airports: being in the middle of people coming and going—being *one* of those people. I'd managed to get past my job placement disappointment by telling myself that Pennsylvania was only a few hours from NYC by train, and returned to thinking of the whole experience as a giant vacation. I dressed accordingly: cute skirt, favorite tank top with bling around the collar, and strappy heels.

As I waited at the gate, I noticed a middle-aged gentleman sitting alone. I'm pretty outgoing, and he seemed like a safe person to talk to, so I sat down nearby and struck up a conversation. I learned he was originally from San Juan, but his job required a lot of travel; at the moment, he was heading home to his family in Pennsylvania. I told him all about myself—including how I ended up with a one-way ticket to Harrisburg. By the time I finished explaining, it was time to board.

I'm an artist, so I kept myself distracted during the flight by drawing. The trip seemed to go by quickly—I guess you could say it "flew by"—and before I knew it, it was time to close my sketchbook and exit the plane.

The moment I stepped into the Pennsylvania airport, strappy heels clacking, I knew something was wrong. I was *freezing*. Shivering and rubbing my arms, I looked around to see if other people were similarly cold, only to be met with the sight of them *totally prepared*—either wearing or carrying heavy winter coats. The man I'd been chatting with earlier sported a light jacket over his royal blue polo shirt, *and* a big winter coat on top of *that*, and slowly it dawned on me: His insulated black boots—so out of place in San Juan—weren't a fashion statement. They were snow boots.

My bare toes looked up at me from within their clacky little sandals, like, OK, *now* what do we do?

The gentleman from San Juan must have guessed at my predicament, because he raised his big, bushy eyebrows and offered to walk me to baggage claim. He asked who was picking me up, and I showed him the paperwork I'd been provided, which included information for a car service. As I hauled my enormous suitcase off the conveyor belt, he gently inquired if I had anything warmer to wear. *Because it was snowing outside.*

"What?!"

Now, let me just say, I'd never seen snow in my entire life. When I thought about October in the United States, I imagined wearing a fun, light sweater of the sort you'd see on *Gilmore Girls*. I opened my suitcase to show my impromptu guardian what I'd packed—he just shook his head.

"Come with me," he said, leading the way to the closest shop inside the airport. I fought back tears, dragging my gigantic bag of useless things, and contemplated calling home, pleading with my parents to please, *please,* rescue me from this (very cold) hell. I was so lost in my thoughts, I didn't notice the gentleman had purchased me a winter coat until he literally put it in my hands. He then offered me a pair of thermal wool socks from his own bag, instructing me to change into a pair of jeans, layer my *Gilmore Girls* sweater under the new coat, and put them on. I was overwhelmed. "Thank you" hardly seemed adequate.

"I have two sons," he told me. "If either one of them were ever in this situation, I'd want someone to help them." Needlessly assuring me the socks were clean, and refusing to accept any money, he instead insisted on waiting with me until my ride arrived. Then he checked the driver's credentials, gave me his phone number in case I got into any trouble, and wished me luck.

Thanks to that paternal stranger, I began my U.S. adventure dressed warmly and feeling a lot less alone. I don't remember his name, but I will never forget the time and care he took to make sure I would be OK.

Also, now I never, ever travel without checking the weather first. ▪

I've Got Your Backpack

ALICIA O.

Before I lost my job in 2019, I'd never been laid off before. I give the experience zero stars, in case you were wondering. Unemployment did not look good on me.

To break up the monotony of job hunting and for a change of scenery, I went to visit my brother in San Francisco. One morning, as we grabbed breakfast at a café in Sausalito, I decided to multitask and applied to some jobs on my laptop. When it was time to leave, I stuffed the computer into my backpack and stood outside, waiting for my brother to pull up the car.

The street in Sausalito was colorful, tree-lined, and full of busy restaurants. I took several minutes to admire my surroundings, thankful that I'd made the decision to visit. This was exactly what I needed. We had a great day sightseeing, and by that evening, my mood was much lighter. Maybe things would be OK, after all.

> How would I apply for jobs? Answer emails? *Restore my life?* I felt like I couldn't do anything right.

But my optimism would not last long. Glancing down at my feet, I realized in absolute horror my backpack was gone. My ID and wallet were in my pocket, but my iPad and laptop were in that backpack. I let out a gasp that nearly sent my brother careening off the road.

"What's wrong?" he asked.

I completely lost my shit, in exactly the way you'd imagine a jobless 29-year-old adult who'd just lost her connection to both the outside world and any potential employment might do. That was the very last straw. How would I apply for jobs? Answer emails? *Restore my life?* I felt like I couldn't do anything right.

We searched the car, called the places we'd visited throughout the day, checked with the police station, and spent almost the entire night searching the streets for my missing backpack. No luck.

I flew back home without it and resigned myself to visiting the public library every day to check my email and set up job interviews. It wasn't ideal, but I was determined to make it work.

About a week after my trip, I got a letter in the mail from a woman named Tara, a manager at the café where we ate breakfast in Sausalito. She'd found my backpack sitting on the curb outside the café. Inside was a voided check, ripped up into little pieces, which she took the time to carefully put back together to get my address.

My brother collected the bag from her and mailed it to me the next day. When it was finally in my hands, I experienced a defining moment: If this could work out for me, then maybe other things would as well.

I called Tara to thank her and let her know that when she returned my bag, she also returned my sense of hope.

I got an amazing job just three months later. ∎

SPOTLIGHT

Last year I was hugely pregnant and got lost on the Tube in London with all my luggage … was crying in public (terrifying for the Brits!). But a kind man asked if I needed help and walked me all the way from the Tube to my destination. When I thanked him, he said, "We all just need to help each other." Then he turned around and went back the same way we came. I'll never forget. —*Gabriela C.*

The Right Accommodation

RANJAN C.

After emigrating from Bangladesh to France in the 1980s, I left to study information technology in London in the '90s. One of the major challenges I faced was finding affordable accommodation. As an overseas student, I had to pay my own fees—unlike domestic British students who had government grants—and there were few flexible jobs for students like me.

I moved from one poor accommodation to the next—five over the course of a year. Most had health hazards and were inadequate and dirty. Walls were damp; black mold lurked in the floors. I'd stay in people's living rooms—arising early each morning to get out of the way and remove the bedding before anyone else woke up. Then, I came across a charitable trust that featured affordable housing for young people moving to London.

I applied and luckily got a room. It was night and day compared with my previous dwellings, and the rent was affordable.

Twenty of us were living in that building. The sense of togetherness, frequent parties, and group activities made me very happy. Out of the 20, only three or four of us knew how to cook, but everyone would make an effort during our potlucks. I remember making spaghetti Bolognese, which went down very well! I think I gained a bit of a reputation, a bit of popularity, once people smelled my cooking coming from the communal kitchen.

The bad news came a year and a half later: The trust had decided to increase the rent. I couldn't afford the increase, and was extremely upset that I had to move out. I'd made friends there, put down roots, and my fellow residents were sad to see me leave. But on the matter of rent, the secretary refused to budge.

So, I went ahead and found a place I could afford: a small room that was probably not legal to live in above a newsagent. It was very damp, with an uncleaned carpet so sticky my shoes would peel right off my feet. No kitchen or shower. No desk to study at. One day, I was chased down by National Front (aka fascist) hooligans for being brown. I'm a fast runner, so I managed to escape. Still, after that, I spent almost all my time in the university library, avoiding my flat as much as possible.

When Jean and Ruth—two friends from my old accommodation—saw how I was living, they took me under their wing as an unofficial adoptee. They were classic cockney East Enders, the building's caretakers, and over 60, with Ruth sporting white hair and Jean flaunting curls.

Both extraordinarily kind and caring, they were always there to help me out. I used to visit them often, have breakfast or tea and toast. When I told them I didn't have a shower in my new quarters, forcing me to rely on the swimming pool changing rooms, Jean and Ruth were aghast, immediately making me promise to use the showers there. *Whenever I wanted,* they assured me, and provided me weekly with clean bedsheets and towels.

In the meantime, to my surprise, a number of residents rallied to my cause and went to see the trust, putting pressure on them to make an exception for me.

After a month and a half, the trust gave in: I was allowed to move back, paying the same rent as before. The sense of solidarity, compassion, and support I experienced touched my heart in a way I honestly can't explain, even now. ■

SPOTLIGHT

I climbed Adam's Peak in Sri Lanka. I was fine going up the mountain, but when I got back down, my legs had totally cramped up and I couldn't walk. A local lady insisted on giving me a full leg massage to ease my pain. She worked wonders! I clearly wasn't the first tourist coming down the mountain she had helped. She wouldn't accept any form of payment, either. —*Zoe J.*

A Christmas Miracle

PALOMA E.

It was late December 2016. I was studying abroad in Iceland and I wanted to get the absolute most out of my time there. My family did, too, so they were flying in from California to spend Christmas with me in Akureyri. I was thrilled to host them. But first, I planned a grand, three-week adventure through the Middle East, timed perfectly between the end of classes and my family's arrival. Or at least that was the plan.

Leaving only a couple days to prepare for my family, I had planned to fly back to Iceland through the international airport in Keflavík, take a bus to the depot in Reykjavík, and then a cab to that airport, where I'd finally return to Akureyri. Ambitious? Possibly. But as I said, I wanted to get the most out of my time abroad. Naturally, once things began going wrong, my ambition began to feel a bit like hubris.

Right out of the gate, my luggage was lost, so I spent about an hour filling out paperwork at Keflavík Airport. Once I found a bus, it was delayed, grinding away more precious time to make my flight out of Reykjavík. Eventually, we were on our way, and after more than 24 hours of travel, the bus pulled into the depot. All I had to do was call a taxi to the airport to make the final leg of my journey. Trouble was, there were no taxis to be had. The ones at the depot were already claimed, and the few services I could contact were too far away.

As time ticked away and busy signals rang in my ears, I kept making progressively grimmer calculations. Maybe if I get one in the next few minutes, and it's very fast, and my plane is delayed …

Flights were being canceled left and right because of the weather, so if I missed mine, who knows how long it would take to get a new one. On top of that, lodging and rebooking might be more than I could afford.

More than anything though, I was simply exhausted. I wanted my bed and 12 hours of sleep. Instead, I began to picture myself stranded here with only the belongings that fit into my carry-on. I pictured my family getting to Akureyri before me and having no clue what to do. I began to picture myself here even longer, with no Christmas and no hope of leaving.

I must have been walking in circles and wearing all of this on my face, because right then, a woman emerged and asked me what was wrong. She asked in English, which was comforting, so everything gushed out at once. Once she understood, she didn't hesitate to offer me a ride. "OK, let's go!" she said. Within minutes, I was in her sedan and on the way to Reykjavík Airport.

> I still don't know what she was doing at the bus depot. She had simply appeared, like a friendly holiday spirit.

I was numb from the cold and sleeplessness, so it took motivation to open up, even for the free ride that was potentially saving my Christmas. The woman asked how I liked Iceland, where I was from, and what I was doing there. I'm sure my answers made less sense than I would have liked. She told me about her daughter, who had visited the U.S. a few years earlier, and how much she had enjoyed it there.

Before I knew it, the woman had dropped me off at the airport. I thanked her profusely, words finally tumbling out all at once, wondering how I could repay the kindness. She simply smiled and said, "Hey, it's Christmas! *Gleðileg jól!*—Merry Christmas!" I still don't know what she was doing at the bus depot. She had simply appeared, like a friendly holiday spirit.

I made my flight in the nick of time, slept at least half a day in my bed, and prepared my home for my family. It was a Christmas to remember—not just because of the location, but also because of what felt like an encounter with an angel, simple though it was.

I really had made the most of my time abroad, but I had hardly done so alone. The flip side of my ambition that year was gratitude. And it was too enormous for words, in any language. ∎

SPOTLIGHT

I was 20 years old and hitchhiking around Europe with a girlfriend from college. Sometimes we stayed in youth hostels; other times we camped. One night in (then) Yugoslavia, we chose to camp in a seedy area, thinking it was a safe spot. Two sisters approached us and, through sign language and broken English, convinced us that this was not a good place to be and that we needed to follow them home.

"Home" turned out to be five people in a one-bedroom, one-bathroom apartment in the local village. The family rearranged themselves to give us the pullout couch. We didn't speak each other's language, but we got a good night's sleep in a stranger's house in a foreign land. As we left, the sisters insisted we accept hand-embroidered doilies to remember them by. We'd never forget them regardless. —*Kim L.*

Hearts and Bows

BECCA S.

T he one thing more challenging than flying across the United States with four children is flying across the United States with four children alone.

My husband and I live in Denver with our kids, a nine-year-old, six-year-old, and four-year-old twins. My mother, whom the kids call Mimi, lives in Virginia. She loves her grandkids, and after a lot of cajoling, she finally convinced me to bring them out to see her last summer. My work schedule is much more flexible than my husband's, which meant that—you guessed it—the kids and I would make the four-and-a-half-hour flight without him, stay for a week, and then fly back home.

Our visit was great—the kids loved seeing all the sights Virginia has to offer, particularly Historic Jamestowne. Mimi was thrilled to take them to a gift shop to get souvenirs, and Dexter, my nine-year-old, selected a bow and arrow replica made from a flimsy piece of wood strung with fishing line. Four arrows came with the bow; the arrowheads were made entirely of leather. The toy was perfect for kids because it was completely harmless. (They could shoot each other in the face without any issues … not that I condoned that!)

On our departure day, it became clear that we were heading home with more stuff than we had arrived with (thanks, Mimi!), so getting everything to fit into our luggage was a challenge. Dexter's arrows fit fine into the checked luggage, but the bow was a problem. I finally decided he would have to carry it onto the plane, which wasn't a big deal; it was light and easy to manage.

After returning the rental car, we made our way to airport security. Each kid had a backpack, a pair of headphones, and an iPad;

Dexter also had his bow. As we began the screening process, the TSA agent tried to confiscate the toy, saying we couldn't board the plane with it.

"Really?" I asked, struggling to keep the irritation out of my voice. "It's only a toy. It's a stick and a string, and we don't have any arrows." Eventually, common sense prevailed, and they let us through after a lot of hemming and hawing.

Relieved, we sat at the gate for about an hour before boarding the plane. I got the kids settled and unpacked, put their seat belts and headphones on, pulled out their iPads, made sure everyone went to the bathroom, and handed them all a snack. We were ready. Just one four-and-a-half-hour flight stood between me and my own bed.

When the plane was fully boarded and ready for takeoff, a gate agent entered the plane and walked up to me. "I need you to get off the plane," he said. "Why?" I asked. He then instructed me to pack up the kids and exit the plane, so I did exactly as I was told, because it had been a long week and I wasn't interested in being arrested in front of my children. The kids were confused and scared, as was I, but I stayed calm and put on a brave face. An entire plane full of passengers watched as we filed off, one by one. When we walked back into the airport, several TSA agents were waiting for us. The kids and I stood in a semi-circle, waiting for an explanation.

The problem was—you guessed it—that damn bow. Again, we went over the fact that it was just a toy and the arrows were in the checked luggage. I asked if we could cut the string, and she said there was simply no way that bow would be allowed on the flight. I could feel my face reddening with anger; frankly, more damage could be done with an iPad than the toy bow. But rules are rules, and these people were not willing to bend them for us. Dexter was horrified, and his siblings' eyes were wide as saucers.

I took a deep breath, centered myself, and asked if we left the bow with them, would we be able to get back on the plane and go home? They said yes, so that's what we did. Dexter handed it over, and we reboarded our flight.

At the bottom of the note, they had one request: "Always remember that most people in the world are nice."

Everyone on the plane clapped for us when we got back on, and as I settled the kids, I told the passengers seated nearby what happened, choosing my words carefully because my children were listening. Poor Dexter was so stressed out! I reassured him, "Dexter, we did not do anything wrong. I am so sorry that we just lost your bow. That bow is not dangerous. I am so shocked and surprised they took it from you." Because honestly, I really was surprised.

A kind couple seated next to us were heading to Denver to visit a new grandchild, and we struck up a conversation. It turned out they knew exactly which gift shop that bow and arrow set had come from, and they insisted on getting our mailing address so they could send us a replacement. It felt crazy, but they eventually convinced me to give it to them. They were grandparents themselves, and they genuinely wanted to help.

Less than a month later, Dexter received a new bow with a beautiful handwritten note that brought tears to my eyes. At the bottom, they had one request: "Always remember that most people in the world are nice."

Dexter was thrilled to have his new bow to go with his arrows, but I was the one that needed the reminder written in the card.

Thank you, Mr. and Mrs. Simmons, for turning what could have been a horrible memory into a beautiful one. ▪

Curly Fries

JOHN V.

I was pretty bummed out. I'd been driving for hours and wasn't much looking forward to the destination.

I was 23 and working for the Coast Guard. I had enlisted three years earlier, just a few months prior to 9/11, and emerged from boot camp two weeks into a war. After training at forts across the country, I was sent to Port Aransas, just south of Corpus Christi, to act as a sea marshal under the newly formed Department of Homeland Security.

The majority of my time there was split between high-risk boardings on incoming foreign ships and search and rescue missions along the Texas coast. The dangers were high, the hours were long, and the sleep nonexistent. We're talking 72-hour on-call shifts, filled with a whole lot of pressure and not much compassion. I'd get homesick often and would visit my parents—nearly a full day's drive north in Erie, Illinois—whenever I could.

I was coming back from one of these visits and still had half a day's journey ahead of me. The night before, I'd slept in my truck as usual and, craving human contact as much as food, I pulled into a diner just outside of Texarkana. I looked awful, but figured I'd be in good company here.

I was sitting at the counter when a man walked in—long black hair, goatee, face full of scruff. He had dirty jeans and a chain wallet: classic trucker vibes through and through. What stuck out to me the most was his shirt: It depicted Curly from the Three Stooges, holding a fork into a light socket. Underneath, it simply read "Curly Fries." Maybe I was delirious from the solitude, but it got me good. I started laughing. "Cool shirt," I told him. We got to chatting.

Everything about me screamed military: Coast Guard shirt, high and tight haircut, zero percent body fat, and a mouth like a sailor. The trucker moved to sit next to me and revealed he was a Vietnam vet. Vets like him loved talking to enlisted guys like me. Barring Desert Storm, most of them hadn't had a chance to feel understood by the generations that came before us. There's a bond there that's difficult to describe, but easy to understand if you're in our shoes. He could tell we were part of the same brotherhood, I guess.

He could also tell that I seemed down. "How you getting back to Corpus Christi?" he asked. I told him I usually took the I-35 to San Antonio, then I-37 east. "Hell no, brother. I've been driving loads down there for years. Let me tell you how to go," he replied, gleam in his eyes. "It's a way better route."

He told me I needed to see the real Texas, not just the interstate. I was game. I grabbed the MapQuest printout from my truck and handed it over, along with a pen. He took his time outlining turn-by-turn directions for me, noting the best restaurants, towns, and miscellaneous sights to take in, all the way to Corpus Christi. It was a humble gesture, but his enthusiasm and care were contagious. I was already feeling less bummed out, even if my 23-hour trip was about to turn into 30.

It was a humble gesture, but his enthusiasm and care were contagious.

My turning point came at the city limits of La Grange. Until then, I'd been contemplative, enjoying the sights but still too aware of what I was driving back to. But something really shifted at La Grange. The ZZ Top song (of the same name, for the uninitiated) was a fave to play on boat patrols, and now here I was, just outside the real McCoy. I took a picture of the sign with my disposable Kodak and hopped back in the truck.

I felt different after that. I noticed the miles and miles of open, untouched land. The deer in the fields, the pastures full of cows. The wild hogs. The enormity of it all, of the state I lived in, took me by surprise for the very first time. I cranked up the music, and a sense of peace washed over me that I still feel to this day. None of this changed the fact that I was now behind schedule, of course. My brain was stressed. But my brain was always stressed. My soul was happy. That was different.

When I finally got back to Port Aransas, I shared the story of "Curly Fries"—the first of many times I'd do so. It was one of the first things I told my wife when I met her in Corpus Christi. I can't even tell you why; I guess it just made me happy and brought back that sense of peace.

Two months after I left the service, my first daughter was born. Her birth was complicated, and she was diagnosed with cerebral palsy. The years that followed were filled with many, many trips to the children's hospital. When you live through something like that, you spend a lot of time looking to the past instead of living in the present. "Curly Fries" was a story, and a feeling, so I went back often. Somehow it even got linked to another song, "Somewhere Down in Texas" by Jason Boland. I'd sing my daughter that song, and inevitably the story would follow. She passed when she was six. But I'd spent her life sharing the feeling of that day with her.

It's a simple thing, to draw a new route for a stranger and shine a light on places they haven't yet considered. It's just as simple to take a leap of faith and follow that route. The result of that exchange is a little more complicated to understand. The trip Curly made for me eventually connected memories, songs, and people as much as it did places. I think of one and then others follow, all colored by that sudden sense of peace. It's become a road map for my mind away from chaos and sadness, straight to a mysterious joy.

Thanks, Curly. ∎

SPOTLIGHT

Got a cold in Istanbul and just wanted to get to my apartment.
Jumped in a taxi.

The driver started talking to me, but we couldn't understand
each other. Suddenly he stopped in a sketchy neighborhood,
jumped out, and went into a store. I got annoyed that he was doing
his personal shopping while I waited in the car and contemplated
whether I should get out and flag another taxi. Suddenly, the driver
returned with a bag full of lemons and some honey. A remedy for
my cold. —*Daniel E.*

About Upworthy

At Upworthy, we're on a mission to share the joy, beauty, and depth of the human experience with every person on the planet. Every day, we amplify stories proving there's good in the world; you just need to know where to look. That's why Upworthy exists: to share the best of humanity. To us, this means bringing people together, being vulnerable, lifting one another up, reflecting love, seeing the best in humankind, standing up for what's right, and making people smile, laugh, and cry.

Upworthy is a gathering place, online and off, for all those who champion the core belief that people are inherently good, and that we have more in common than not. Founded in 2012, it reaches 100 million people a month through various channels across social media, web, and email.

Join us @upworthy on all platforms.

Acknowledgments

Creating this book was an undertaking that wouldn't have been possible without drawing upon the deep well of support from so many people in our lives. We'd like to extend our deepest gratitude to all those who helped us complete this journey. Your support has been immeasurable.

An enormous thank-you to every person whose lives form the backbone of this book. Each one of your experiences is a testament to the beauty of the human spirit. We feel privileged that you've shared your stories with us, so that we can in turn share them with the world. We know that all who read them will be moved, inspired, and comforted by them, just as we have been.

And thank you to every single person who is part of the Upworthy community. We exist because of you and appreciate you.

To our head writer, Rachel Reilich, whose talent with words and ability to understand and unearth the truths of the human experience breathed life into this entire collection: Thank you. To our tireless team of writers (some of whom were contributors themselves!)—Harmony Hobbs, Iris Ng, Royce Johnson, Micaela Macagnone, Audrey Wachs, Heather Wake, Susan Johnston Taylor—you transformed what started as a few short lines into beautiful, true, first-person short stories—some hilarious, others heart-wrenching, all human. Thank you for climbing this 60,000-word mountain with us. We couldn't have done this without you.

To our literary agent, Emma Parry, for championing this idea of ours since day one. Your guidance, instincts, and wisdom have centered us throughout this entire process. We're so grateful. Thank you to Melissa Flashman, a dear friend and our bridge to Emma and the entire team at Janklow & Nesbit.

We couldn't have imagined better publishing partners than the team at National Geographic and Disney. To our editor, Hilary Black, your enthusiasm for this book has lifted our spirits and instilled a sense of confidence in us. Elisa Gibson, your design sensibility makes each page sing. Gabriela Capasso, your dedication to managing the nuts and bolts of this project is so appreciated. And special thanks to Libby VanderPloeg for bringing these amazing stories to life through your beautiful illustrations. They're the best.

To the team at GOOD Worldwide—Sammi Mo, Noemi Salcedo, Jessica Laufer, Naomi Yasuda, Timothy Porter, Kiron Chakraborty, Maria Henriquez, Tatiana Cardenas, Mindy Nguyen, Eric Pfeiffer (and the whole editorial team), and, of course, Max Schorr—your unwavering support during this process has made all the difference. Thank you.

From Lucia:

To my family, my lifeboat before, during, and after this winding, life-altering journey, you never wavered once. I feel so lucky to have such a dynamic bunch of whip-smart, weird, funny, and deeply empathetic humans as my bloodline. I love each of you as individuals and together.

To my brother, Dwight Knell, I wrote a story about you and now it's published. That's cool. But really you did that. Thank you, Dwiggy. I literally could not have done this without you.

To my devoted and loving parents, Kim Larson and Gary Knell, thank you for showing me what it means to be there, no matter what. The ardent support you've shown me over the past year is something I'll carry with me for the rest of my life. I love you.

To my stunning sisters, Maya Knell, Savannah Knell, and Jillian Lenson (My, Nanny, and Gwillers). Queer icons, slays, etc. You consistently remind me that I, too, am a slay. Thank you, queens.

To my 100-year-old feminist grandmother, Barbara Peters, who has bravely blazed a trail for women since the 1930s and inspires me constantly.

To the people who showed up in ways I couldn't have imagined:

Leah Sack, Jenny Poretz, Genevieve Uslander, Gabby Gonzalez, Myra Sack, Ollie LaViolette, Jess Wolinsky, Beth Sosin, and Ted Poretz. I cherish you.

And to Danielle Kayne-O'Gilvie, thank you for buoying me through all kinds of waters and keeping things in perspective. I am here because of you.

Lastly, to my cat, Millie. Thanks for the cuddles.

From Gabriel:

To my love, Modesta Zapata—you allow me to see things clearly and stay centered when I desperately need to. Your emotional and spiritual support (including with this book) means more to me than I can put in words.

To my dad, Reid Reilich, the best person I've ever known. You showed me how to love people and the world—I miss you every day.

To my courageous and brilliant mom, Danielle Reilich, you taught me the importance of having a strong moral compass. Your lessons have guided me through life, and for that I'll be forever grateful.

To my sisters, Rachel and Jessica, you've been helping me succeed and been there to lift me up my entire life. I love you both so much.

To my grandmother, Bella Feniger, your strength and resilience will always inspire me.

To my space brother, Tyler Brock—thanks for being there for me since kindergarten. Your support means the world to me.

To Rick Dierker, the wizard, you opened my eyes to the magic in the world. You were there for me when I needed it most.

To Dan Dengrove, Daniel Hatkoff, and Danny Marshall— you're the best Dans a guy could ever ask for.

To my friends, colleagues, and compatriots who've helped me on this journey—Tommy, McKinley, Jamie, Lakis, Holly, Andy, Anna, Sean, Ryan, and so many more—you are the best.

And to my dog, Totem, for always reminding me what really matters in life: food, friends, and the outdoors.

About the Editors

Gabriel Reilich

Gabriel Reilich is the head of content and innovation at Upworthy, where he has worked since 2014. Devoted to his mission of spreading optimism, he believes the internet can be a force for good, and is dedicated to leveraging it to amplify the best of humanity. Throughout his career, he has created content and crafted impact campaigns for numerous respected brands, nonprofits, and nongovernmental organizations such as Google, GoFundMe, and the World Food Programme. He is a fan of looking for cool rocks, listening to classic country music, and perfecting puns. A native of Los Angeles, he graduated with honors from UC Berkeley with a B.A. in political science. He lives in Los Angeles.

Lucia Knell

Lucia Knell is the vice president of brand at Upworthy, where she's worked since 2014. She's spent her career championing the belief that the internet can and should be used as a tool to unite people rather than stoke division. Her expertise in social media has garnered millions of engagements and catalyzed a movement to combat negativity online. An ardent advocate for mental health, she also believes in the power of taking breaks from the internet. Her work has been covered in the *New York Times, Glamour, Vogue, Fast Company,* and the mental health publication *Made of Millions.* Originally from New York, she is a proud cum laude graduate of Kenyon College in Gambier, Ohio, with a B.A. in Spanish literature. She is a dancer, choreographer, and FM radio enthusiast, and she enjoys cheering people on at marathons. She splits her time between Los Angeles and New York City.